"Here's your number. Remember that.
You ain't got a name anymore."

Prisoner 11841, recalling advice from a guard.

Numbered

Inside Idaho's Prison for Women, 1887-1968

Edited by Todd Shallat and Amber Beierle

IDAHO STATE HISTORICAL SOCIETY

Boise, Idaho 2020

ASSOCIATE EDITOR:
Colleen Brennan

GRAPHIC DESIGNER:
Toni Rome, Guy/Rome

ILLUSTRATOR:
Kelly Knopp

RESEARCH ASSOCIATES:
Jacey Brain
Skye Cranney
Hayley Noble
Anthony Parry
Royce Williams

ISBN: 978-0-931406-17-1
Copyright © 2020

IDAHO STATE
**HISTORICAL
SOCIETY**

history.idaho.gov

About the cover: Ida Laherty, a horse thief, convicted at age 16 in 1903, ignited moral outrage over prisons where women and children served time among dangerous men.

Left: *Edna Eckersley*, by Beth Suter, 2018. Previous: Emily May McLaws (Idaho State Historical Society [ISHS]); the Women's Ward (Alamy). Following pages: Idaho State Penitentiary Administration Building (ISHS); Women's Ward flanks the warden's house, 1950s (ISHS); bottom: Idaho inmates tend the ward's garden, prepare a meal, and sew, 1950s (ISHS).

Contents

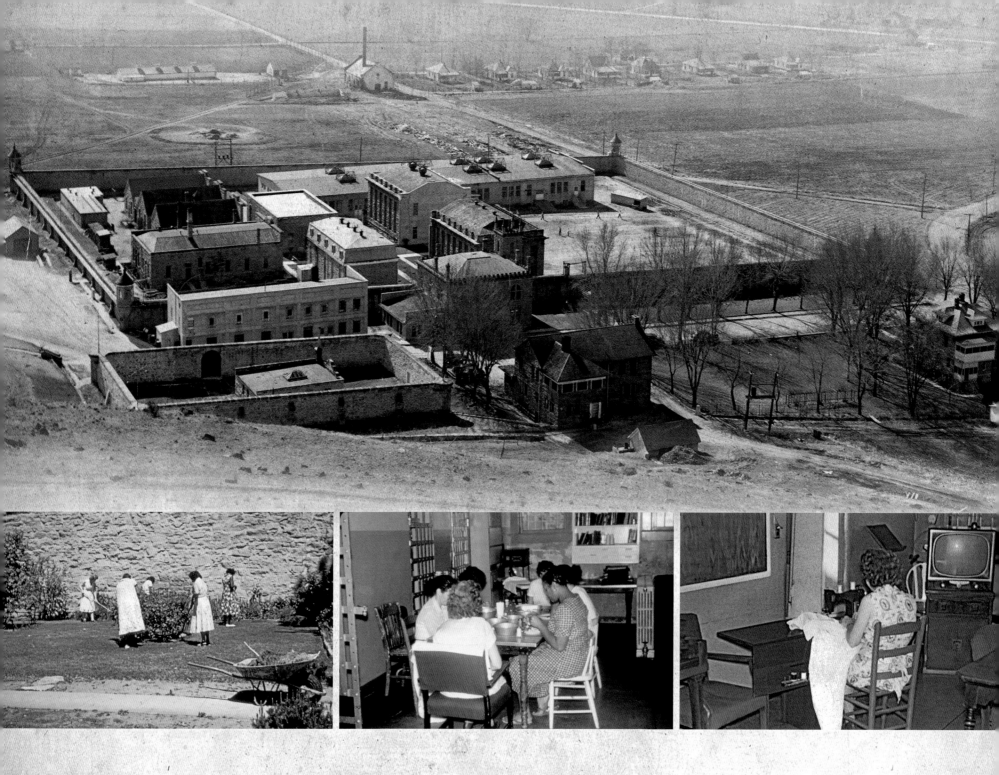

Foreword

Numbered explores the harsh realities of challenging times for 216 Idaho women. From 1887 to 1968, from territorial times to the closing of the women's cellblock, all were wards of the state serving time as convicted inmates at the Idaho State Penitentiary, now a national historic site. The book project emerged from a statewide effort to honor the 100th anniversary year of the 19th Amendment to the U.S. Constitution, a law that extended women's suffrage, establishing national voting rights. We join that commemoration with a reminder that women from all walks of life — even those on society's margins — face life-changing social and political struggles. Their Idaho stories contribute to the rich complexity of the collective history that colors our lives.

Executive Director, Idaho State Historical Society

Women stood arm-in-arm with prison reformers in the hard-fought campaign for equal protection under the law. Twenty-four years before national women's suffrage, in 1896, Idahoans had taken the lead with an amendment to the state's constitution that granted women the vote. Pictured: Women march for suffrage, 1913.

SOURCE: LIBRARY OF CONGRESS

1

Women, Crime, and Doing Time

If a woman's place was the home, if her virtue was pious and frail,
what kind of beast was the woman who strayed?

By Todd Shallat, with Amber Beierle

Mugshots haunt like phantoms in a jailhouse séance, the living seeking the dead. Inmate 565, age 25, curly headed and elfish, sits for the jailer's camera in a puffy dress of layered gingham, her eyes fixed with the inky stare of a widow who seems dumbfounded to be caught with her husband's corpse. Inmate 3542, called a "dope fiend" by the prosecutor, bobs her hair like a Jazz Age flapper. Inmate 2563, convicted of rape, glares with bitter defiance. Inmate 3281, a bootlegger, scowls.

"Here's your number," said the guard after snapping the mugshot. "Remember that. You ain't got a name anymore. Anytime you come and go, you give the number."

From 1887 to 1968 in Boise, below a natural mesa called Table Rock, 216 women were numbered and mugshot as involuntary wards of the state. Nearly all shared a stout little sandstone cellblock in the shadow of the male prison. The Women's Ward, it was called. Seven tiny double-occupancy cells opened into a concrete dayroom. Built with convict labor, its stone cut from the quarry a mile east of the site, the ward stood 18 feet by 20 feet, behind a 17-foot outer wall. No guard tower commanded the cellblock. No buzzers or bulletproof glass.

"Our ward is rather small," wrote Nancy "Chris" Christopher in 1960. Three years earlier, she had used chairs and a table to scale the garden's perimeter wall.

So few were the crimes, so frequent the pardons, that the solid little cellhouse stood nearly empty at times. From 1906 to 1968, during the 62-year active life of the cellblock, the bouncing and forging of checks were the most common of female crimes. Thirteen months was the average sentence. Five days was the shortest. Nineteen years, the longest. Six inmates were the most admitted in any one year before the crime wave of the Great Depression. By 1965, however, the Women's Ward had overcrowded, and health officials began to demand that the cellblock be permanently closed.

Today, per capita, Idaho ranks fifth in the nation in females incarcerated. The state's population of female offenders grows at double the rate for men. Looking backward, the contrast is stark. Suspended between then and now, between the eras of the

A small plank house once used by the warden became the kitchen and washroom for women prisoners in 1906.
SOURCE: IDAHO STATE HISTORICAL SOCIETY (ISHS)

A 17-foot wall of Table Rock sandstone boxed in the 1906 women's annex. In 1920, an addition with seven double-occupancy cells fronted a dayroom.
SOURCE: ISHS

Victrola and iPhone, is the history of separate but decidedly unequal gender treatment by Idaho courts of law. A morality tale, it is the story of a double standard — for women, the strictest purity; for men, the freedom to carouse and indulge. The history of lives in confinement is also about race and class. Then as now, among men and women, African Americans, Native Americans, and Hispanics

The 1860s Idaho gold rush brought nine men for every woman. In 1896, the year of Idaho women's suffrage, men still outnumbered women four to one.

were overrepresented. So were the transient, the paupered, the battered, the broken, the inebriated, and the drug addicted. Few left behind memoirs or mausoleums. But their lives, if we listen, astonish us. Faintly we can hear them still in their cold confinement where vacant faces in graying mugshots whisper through concrete walls.

Gender and Justice

Women, even fallen women, numbered few in the Idaho gold camps. The 1870 territorial census showed nine men for every woman. Prostitution flourished. If the sinned against was also pronounced a sinner, if she was violent or her depravity was deemed extreme, that wayward soul might languish in a county jail. Stella Richards of Boise frequented jail in Ada County but saw no penitentiary time. In 1886, in a drunken terror on Main Street, she brained an officer of the court with a beer glass. Four years later in Nampa, a prostitute named Nettie Bowen screamed, "You son of a bitch, I will kill you now" before shooting her brothel's landlord. The bullet pierced the man's right arm, then bounced off the buckle of his suspender. Bowen's punishment was $100 in fines.

The double-edged sword of that double standard was dependency in the extreme. "Let women learn in silence with all subjection" was a Bible verse frequently quoted. Susan B. Anthony, the suffragist, an inspiration to Protestant temperance ladies in

Boise and Pocatello, saw rote biology in the origin of crime. For men, said Anthony in the 1880s, the motive was "love of vice." For women, it was "destitution." A woman, unlike a man, could be morally rehabilitated. Idealized, she was a flower too frail for back-breaking physical labor, too submissive for public floggings, too pious and pure and timid to commit the most heinous of crimes.

Men were another story. Forty thousand were jailed or imprisoned in territories and the 35 states at the close of the Civil War. Sixteen at once were chained by the legs in the boomtown of Idaho City where a pine log cabin was the territory's original jail. The porous log jail was a "farce," said the *Idaho Tri-Weekly Statesman*. On

January 22, 1867, Congress authorized $40,000 for a proper territorial prison with sentries and cellblocks. It would be in Boise City within a bugle's call of the sabers and combines of the capital's cavalry post. Legend has it that the City of Lewiston, Boise's rival, agreed to the Table Rock penitentiary site in exchange for the promise of the University of Idaho. Idahoans still dispute who got the better deal.

In 1870 construction began about two miles east of Boise under the quarry that provided the stone. Two years later the first prisoners arrived. "The prison looms up like the frowning walls of some impregnable fortress," wrote the *Idaho Statesman* as the masons chiseled the sandstone. In 1888 another $25,000 from Congress underwrote a second wing of 42 cells. By 1895, again overcrowded, the prisons had 153 inmates, all but one of them male.

A glass-plate photograph from 1894 shows Idaho's dark architecture of brooding regimentation: heavy arches, castle battlements, stone turrets with conical roofs, plank catwalks for guards with rifles and shotguns, an entry hallway with doors massive enough to withstand an artillery shelling. A three-story tower spires skyward in the Romanesque style of a fortress bastille. Black-hatted Warden John P. Campbell turns stiffly back toward the camera in the photograph's foreground. In the distance, faintly, is a modest house that was later remodeled and became the Women's Ward.

The setting, in its broken volcanic starkness, was sacred to some. It was here during the Indian wars that a Shoshone woman tended to the sick and wounded with steaming water from healing springs; here also that trapper Donald McKenzie saw smoke signals from Table Rock; here again that prisoners breaking rock found beaded skeletons in an ancient boneyard; and here a century later that the City of Boise purchased a yellow hillside to ward off a subdivision. In 1956, above the prison on the lip of the mesa, the Boise Jaycees erected a 60-foot electrified cross. A decade passed before the federal

Warden John P. Campbell in a snowy field outside the newly expanded Idaho State Penitentiary, 1894.
SOURCE: ISHS

courts began to sour on public monuments to any one religion. In 1971, the Idaho Department of Corrections quietly retroceded four square feet at the base of the cross to the care of churches and service clubs.

Male prisoners quarried the stone used for the penitentiary and public buildings such as the Idaho Statehouse.

No woman who was white and Christian served time below the contested mesa before the decade of Idaho statehood. Before 1890, the lone female inmate was a Bannock Indian convicted of killing her husband. Henebe, age 27, had no surviving full name or mugshot. In 1887 she climbed a fence and escaped. Recaptured, her sentence commuted, she served a year of her three-year sentence.

The first female who was white and Christian was deranged. Margaret Hardy of Latah County, age 48 in 1895, had murdered her adopted daughter, burning out the child's eyes with carbonic acid.

Table Rock Cross, reflected in the diamond window above the entrance to the penitentiary's dining hall.
SOURCE: STEVE BARRETT

Kensler's hound dog led investigators to the sunken corpse of his master.

"Black Hearted Old Hag" was the headline in the *Idaho Statesman*. Prison guards did what they could, providing furniture, heating a sunlit cell with a furnace in the penitentiary's hospital ward. Guards remembered Hardy crouched on the floor with a venomous grin, screaming, sobbing, and laughing. She ate glass. She set fire to bed clothes. Visits to the dungeon's "bughouse" had no apparent effect. "Her sex alone saved her from hanging," said a *Statesman* reporter. Six months and 18 days into Hardy's prison sentence, a board of doctors booked her passage to Blackfoot's hospital for the insane.

Hardy, a tempest, foreshadowed a media cyclone of sexual innuendo from a second female inmate who landed the following year. The "hurricane with hazel eyes" was how the *Statesman* later recalled the chaos. Before the storm subsided, powerful men were indicted, a governor was tossed from office, and the prison's double standard was reasserted to untangle gender lines.

Josie Kensler, that hazel-eyed brewing cyclone, was a Malad farm girl of 14 when sent to Elmore County to marry an older rancher. At age 24 in 1896, a mother of two, she took to harvesting hay with a brutish young ranch hand named Alfred Freel. One violent Saturday night in October, Kensler — or possibly Freel — used the rancher's own .45 carbine to shoot him while he snored in his bed. Kensler and Freel found a ditch nearby for the body. Hitching a wagon, they crashed it on the banks of the Snake River so that it looked as if its driver had been pitched into the river. But the family hound knew better. Returning each day to the ditch that held his murdered master, the dog flopped on his belly and scratched at a thin patch of ice. In December, two months after the shooting, deputies dredged the ditch with a crowbar. Up came the head-shot corpse. Soon a search of the ranch house produced the widow's bare bloody footprint and a bullet hole in a bed. Freel was convicted of murder. Kensler, her jury in tears, got murder in the second degree.

"If it hadn't been for that dadblasted dog," the *Statesman* reported, mocking the crime.

On May 28, 1897, Boiseans gathered at the 10th Street depot for a glimpse of the pale young celebrity convict. Five-foot-five and "a beauty," according to male reporters, Kensler was "a dark-haired siren with a yearning to exploit her assets." The warden Charles Van Dorn had a barber shop converted to a furnished cell with a new feather mattress. A part-time female matron was hired. "[Van Dorn] thinks she will not be troublesome and will submit," said the *Statesman*. Submit she did, but not in the way the warden expected. Already on her arrival the widow was six months pregnant. Three months later a newborn daughter was entrusted to a sister-in-law.

Five years into Kensler's sentence, the storm reached hurricane force. New warden Charles E. Arney, formerly a probate judge, had been rewarded for political service with the state's sweetest patronage plum. Politics also paved a path for prison physician Jesse K. Dubois, whose younger brother in the U.S. Senate represented the 43rd state. In July 1902, the widow confronted the warden and his physician. Shocking them both with a dangerous secret, she demanded a quid pro quo. Kensler, somehow, was pregnant. The warden, she offered, could arrange for her immediate pardon, or he could face corruption charges and reserve a prison cell for himself.

"It [the pregnancy] will kill me politically," said Arney to the prison's turnkey. "Get rid of it" was the doctor's advice. Pills were prescribed. A miscarriage followed. Kensler filed charges in Ada County through an attorney. Warden and doctor were indicted for conspiring to induce an abortion, a capital crime.

"Sensation at the Penitentiary," blared the *Statesman* headline, September 3, 1902. "Warrants Issued for the Arrest of Warden Arney and Prison Physician Dubois on Committing an Abortion." An editorialist said there was "no greater disgrace" than to confine a woman among lustful men.

Warden Arney flatly denied it. Pregnancy was inconceivable because, said Arney, the widow was too closely watched. Dubois meanwhile claimed that his pills were but a tonic to calm a poor woman's nerves. Both defendants won over their juries, but the storm was far from over. Investigators looking at prison ledgers found "deficiencies" totaling $7,522 (perhaps $220K today). Prison cattle and "most anything not nailed down" had been found in Owyhee County on the warden's private ranch. "The bad odor of mismanagement smells to heaven," said the *Lewiston Teller*. Arney was forced to resign. Voters responded five weeks later in statewide elections that booted Arney's patrons from power.

Kensler served seven more years under Table Rock. Released in 1909, she remarried to a theater owner, spending her days scrubbing his floors. Two years later she fled. "Goodbye, I am leaving," said the note to her jilted husband. She had eloped, it was said, with a recently pardoned convict, leaving the state but taking her gun.

Left: Penitentiary physician Jesse Dubois. Pennyroyal tablets commonly used to induce an abortion, about 1900.
SOURCE: ISHS, ANTICURIA.COM

Below: Warden Charles Arney, 1901.
SOURCE: ISHS

17

Necessary to Isolate

The *affaire de Kensler* confirmed the absolute necessity of impregnable walls to isolate female convicts. Idaho in the year of the miscarriage scandal was one of only three American states without a separate cellblock for women. Elsewhere in the nation — notably Massachusetts, also in New York and Indiana — wardens and their prison commissions had strived to "naturalize" the architecture of incarceration, removing the gray and metallic, adding gardens and hearths. Bedspreads and linens softened time in confinement. Song and prayer, the faithful believed, would hush the fallen women into quiet submission. Moral therapy would rekindle, in the hardest of hearts, a respect for virtue and the pious life.

But Idaho's numbers remained too small for social experimentation. Before 1906, only 12 female convicts had served state penitentiary time. Six had listed their occupation as "housekeeper." Four were orphans. Four were from Missouri. Three were African Americans. One had late-stage tuberculosis. Another was a mystery without a mugshot, called "inhuman" for her grim appearance. She was a felon without family and "utterly deserted," said a court reporter. Not a friend on Earth had uttered a word on her behalf.

It was the youngest of the 12 female convicts who incited the loudest protest. Ida Laherty of Moscow was only 16. Fatherless, white, and Catholic, she had been caught across state lines with her boyfriend's team of stolen horses. Guards called her an "ill-mannered child." Boise's Woman's Christian Temperance Union (WCTU), a powerful lobby, called her a scandal waiting to happen. WCTU petitions and vigils forced the teenager's transfer to a private home. Lawmakers then enacted a statute that empowered the state to parole any juvenile convict regardless of gender or crime.

Laherty and her sisters in isolation spanned an anguished decade of mourning for the green republic lost to industrialization. Evangelicals called it an epoch of "the social gospel," its emphasis on earthly salvation, on freeing children from factory labor and cleansing the great unwashed. Historians have come to call it the Era of Progressive Reform. A morality crusade, a political movement, it targeted mostly the rough immigrant men from Catholic places where demon rum still haunted the bawdy houses. White slavery (prostitution), venereal disease, and rehabilitation for female felons were also burning concerns. Reformers in Idaho pitched ballots for women as sober resistance to the Catholic Democrat vote. Equal suffrage also drew strength from the same demographic imbalance that kept women imprisoned with men. "There are at least four men to every woman in this State," the *Wood River Times* reported in 1896 on the eve of the suffrage vote. "If we recognize the right of women to suffrage, we will soon get an increase in population that will help us all."

Right: The 1903 conviction of Ida Laherty, age 16, prompted a law to expedite pardons for minors.
SOURCE: ISHS

Below: A temperance cartoon. Temperance reformers blamed alcohol for the enslavement of women and crusaded for prison reform.
SOURCE: VIRGINIA COMMONWEALTH UNIVERSITY LIBRARIES

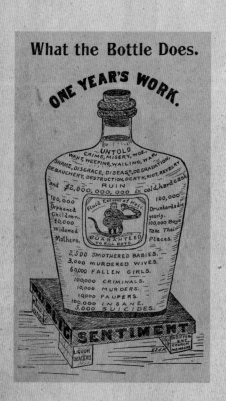

On November 3, 1896, in a festive riot of flowering hats and political bunting, the Gem State became fourth in the nation to grant women a constitutional right to the vote. Politically, it was a vital moment both more and less than it seemed. Suffrage, more than symbolic, boosted statewide campaigns for temperance and child welfare. Suffrage also meant power for Latter-day Saints in southeastern Idaho precincts, where mothers and daughters outnumbered solitary unmarried men. But women's suffrage, less than it seemed, fell short of what many had hoped and promised. It did not translate to equal rights in business and property law. It did not grant a mother equal claim to the custody of her children. It did not stop a husband from beating his wife.

Fear that suffrage would not be enough — that women might also want to serve on juries and in the Idaho Statehouse, marching in lockstep dour formation against male intemperance and lust — stirred a political backlash that tempered Progressive reform. In 1899, for example, a drunkard named William McGraw appealed his rape conviction, blaming his plight on "the female vote." McGraw lost his appeal, but the protest resonated. The rare brave woman who volunteered for a jury was often mocked by a judge. In 1924, in a throwback decision called *State v. Kelley*, the Idaho State Supreme Court insisted that "a jury was a body of *men*" and that a man convicted by women had legitimate grounds for appeal.

Male incarceration, meanwhile, outpaced Idaho's population. From 1896 to 1906, from 128 inmates to 220, the state's prison population nearly doubled. Warden Eugene L. Whitney did what he could for the women. During the dry winter of 1905-1906, with convict labor and surplus hardware, the prison pieced together a small free-standing women's compound under the northwest rifleman's tower. A squarish blockhouse flanked a small plank house to be used as a kitchen. Narrow berms of dusty yard were marked off for flower gardens. Prison-grade steel gated two points of entry through a tall rectangular wall.

Left: Idaho women's suffrage umbrella, 1896.
SOURCE: NATIONAL MUSEUM OF AMERICAN HISTORY

Collier's magazine imagined a future with women serving on juries, 1903.
SOURCE: LIBRARY OF CONGRESS

Criminologists studied the biology of deviance with experiments on female offenders. Suffragettes protested the torture. Pictured: Torturing women in prison, 1909.

SOURCE: NATIONAL WOMEN'S SOCIAL AND POLITICAL UNION

On June 19, 1906, with little fanfare, the *Statesman* reported the opening of "a neat stone structure," calling it the "women's annex." Warden Whitney hired his wife as a matron to watch over Kensler and four other female convicts. The women now did their own laundry and cooked daily meals. Soon, Whitney boasted, they would be washing and sewing for men.

Profiling the Criminal Mind

Whitney's ward for wayward women laid bare the in-between shadowy nature of the felon's mercurial place. If biology was destiny, if the fairer sex was God's favored gender in the progress of civilization, then what was the woman who strayed? Physicians at the University of Turin in the 1880s and 1890s searched for answers by pricking women with needles and reading the bumps on their heads. Cesare Lombroso's *La Donna Delinquente* (1893) theorized that the female offender was an "atavistic" throwback to a more primitive breed of apelike humanoid creatures. Their small craniums with sloping foreheads marked their congenital defects. So did jutting jaws, jug ears, hawk noses, colorblindness, and numbness to pain. Prostitutes were likely obese, according to this Darwinian science. Deviants, often left-handed, were prone to epilepsy. Female killers had a glassy stare in their bloodshot eyes.

But Lombroso's theory was hard to square with the women living under Table Rock. French, Mexican, Nez Perce, Swedish, Irish, Mormon, and Baptist, they were a jumble more diverse than the state's population. The shortest was 4 feet 9 inches, the tallest 5 feet 11 inches, the smallest 93 pounds, the largest 240 pounds. Multiracial and multilingual, they

were "organisms responding and reacting to various [environmental] stimuli," said the criminologist Frances Kellor, writing in 1901. Kellor considered head bumps incidental to the mind-bending power of capitalism's social decay. Physical abuse, sexual exploitation, poor education, low wages, and the tedium of menial jobs were said to be preconditions of female criminal recidivism. Alcohol and narcotics also bred criminal lives.

To Kellor goes much of the credit for coining "underclass" as a word to explain the toxic symbiosis of poverty, minority status, and poor education that became the common social markers of life on the bottom rail.

Low wages for tedious work, an important predictor according to Kellor, was one of the few quantifiable measures of underclass status in Idaho's inmate files. From 1908 to 1968, of the Women's Ward's 211 inmates, four out of five were listed as housekeeper, housewife, or "unknown." There were also waitresses (36 inmates), cooks (9), nurses (9), farm laborers (5), clerks (3), bar maids (3), a beautician, and a potato sorter. Sixty-seven inmate files linked delinquency to vagrancy or extreme financial distress.

Phrenology, the science of reading bumps on the head, was thought to be the key to understanding criminal behavior in women, about 1890.

Left: Italian criminologist Cesare Lombroso blamed female delinquency on congenital defects, 1893.

SOURCE: INTERNETARCHIVE.ORG

21

Poverty and abuse tipped the scales of justice against the most vulnerable Idahoans. Pictured: Impoverished Idaho migrants, Oneida County, 1936.
SOURCE: U.S. FARM SECURITY ADMINISTRATION

Prohibition-era bootlegger, about 1925.
SOURCE: LIBRARY OF CONGRESS

Today, by comparison, the National Institute of Justice has cited poverty and poor education as the strongest predictors of criminal recidivism, crippling 79 percent of women in prisons and jails.

Race was another factor. Significantly, with only 3 percent of the state's population listed as nonwhite in Idaho's midcentury census, 21 percent of the Women's Ward inmates were categorized as Native American, African American, or Mexican. Among the Native Americans, mostly Shoshone and Nez Perce, the words "drunkenness," "dope," and/or "narcotics" appear in 21 of 23 inmate files.

Especially vulnerable were the 60-plus penitentiary women convicted of forging or writing bad checks. Many were single mothers with hungry children — in Pocatello, for example, where French immigrant Sarah Bradley forged checks to feed four children; in Twin Falls, where Ruth Haynes, mother of five, floated checks to cover her disabled son's hospitalization; in Lewiston, where Lola Hewett promised to make restitution on a $20 grocery check. Credit card fraud ensnared Emily May McLaws, who was offered parole but had nowhere to go. All were women who fit Kellor's description of "restricted activity" in farm-based economies with few escape routes for unmarried women.

Likewise it was minor offenses for petty sums that overwhelmed Barbara Singleton, a four-time repeat offender, who listed her occupation as housewife and repeatedly kited checks throughout Twin Falls County. Court documents implicate an abusive husband on probation for the same offense.

Not everyone was impoverished — not the clerk embezzler from a Boise family of standing; not the madam arrested for bootlegging or the deputy county treasurer who skimmed $9,000 to cover her gambling debts. Of the 30 most violent offenders, those convicted of murder or manslaughter after 1906, there were 13 with criminal files that mentioned extreme financial hardship. Another eight were listed as housewives.

Both the rich and the poor won pardons. "This is due to the sympathy and consideration which men give women," Kellor explained. Five months of a 10-year maximum sentence earned the governor's pardon for Flossie Phillips of Lincoln County, who, in 1940, had helped her brothers hog-tie their father, leaving him in the desert to die. For Caddie Shupe of Montpelier, convicted of shooting her lover, the promise to return to her husband was quid pro quo for reducing her sentence by half. For Margaret Brooks of Montana, who tossed her infant from a fast-moving train, a year and a month was enough. Lyda Southard, aka Lady Bluebeard, served about four years per murdered husband. Of Idaho's 37 women convicted of murder and manslaughter, 1887 to 1968, only four served more than 10 years.

Paroles and pardons seemed to be Idaho's way of conceding that many a violent offender had been fighting off a drunken man. Jeannette Benoy of Idaho County, age 65, served two-and-a-half years for blasting a boozed-up husband who was beating

her with an iron bar. An African American cook from Twin Falls named Mary Turner Hansom sat for her 1936 mugshot with an eye welted shut from a beating. Convicted of killing her husband, Hansom had shot him, she said, "on accident" in an era of victimization about 50 years before battered woman syndrome became a legal defense.

Brawls that sent women to prison usually ended with a smoking handgun. Frances Ernst of Valley County, age 36, had used a pistol to stop dead a fight between a jealous ex-husband and a lusting neighbor. When the husband confessed to the shooting, Ernst emerged from hiding to volunteer her own confession. She appears to have been one of only two women in the sandstone cellblock for its 1920 renovation. Cells now had steam heat, electric lights, flush toilets, and bunkbeds. There was a whitewashed dayroom with a Victrola and woven rugs but very few inmates. Not until 1937 were more than five women in shared confinement. Not until 1954 did the seven-cell ward reach its double-occupancy cell capacity of 14.

In December 1960 the arrival of a 15th inmate forced an inmate to sleep in the dayroom. "The more the merrier," wrote Nancy "Chris" Christopher, reporting for Idaho's one and only penal publication, a newspaper called *The Clock*. "What are we going to do if more guests come? There are several of us here who I am sure would be more than glad to relinquish their space to some more deserving person. I suppose, and if necessary, we can always resort to three-tiered bunks."

Fifteen women with little to do sometimes made time for mischief. A prison hooch called "squawky," also called raison jack, pruno, or brew, challenged the thirsty to imbibe while holding their noses. Coffee grounds and bread yeast were fermented into foul concoctions.

Another amusing annoyance was the teasing and flashing of men. In 1966 a volleyball game turned raucous when a woman, retrieving a ball, climbed on the roof to yoo-hoo a red-shirted male inmate. A

A Women's Ward cell and (left) the dayroom, 1950s.
SOURCE: ISHS

Men were the builders of bridges and railroads. Women, childlike, were said to be timid, submissive, and chaste. Pictured: Genteel ladies play tennis at the warden's residence beneath the penitentiary's tower, about 1900.

SOURCE: ISHS

visit from the warden followed. "We don't like having you here any more than you like being here," said Warden Louis E. Clapp, a veteran of 22 years. "I wish you would learn to behave like ladies. Ladies don't get on top of a building and wave."

But ladylike behavior in the 1960s was not what it was in 1906. Women now sat as judges and jurors, and many were less forgiving than men. Second-wave feminism took on marital rape, unequal pay, and discriminatory custody laws. In 1968, the year the Women's Ward folded, protesters burned bras and marched against the Miss America Beauty Pageant. Pop-culture B-movie classics — *So Evil, So Young* was one, 99 *Women* another — fetishized the female offender as butch and sadistic. "Women in prison [are] looked upon as hard and cold as steel," Christopher explained in *The Clock*. "The sister is ashamed to be with you. The agency sees you as a woman who has lost the right to be a mother. Then the heartache comes. It is like a giant hammer beating on a molten mass."

On July 1, 1968, after 62 years, the Women's Ward officially closed. Four prisoners topped out their time at women's prisons in Oregon and Nevada. Another generation would pass before Idaho reclaimed its own at the Pocatello Women's Correctional Center, opened in 1994.

Visiting the Past

The Sixties rocked the world in which women, if Christian and white, were routinely dismissed as too passive and soft to be hardened in prison like men. The gender divide had shifted with American

jurisprudence. Fading was the chivalry factor that made policemen with female suspects think twice before making arrests.

"If women want to be treated equally, fine, we'll punish them equally," said Bertha Josephson, an attorney with the American Civil Liberties Union, suing Kentucky over prison conditions in 1982. "Unfortunately the punishment [for women] turns out to be more severe in certain respects."

Hollywood fetishized women in prison with scenes of catfights and voyeurism.

SOURCE: AMERICAN INTERNATIONAL PICTURES

Numbers tell some of that story. The 20th century ended with one of every 109 women in America living in the U.S. correctional system. Idaho, by 1999, had doubled the capacity of its women's prison to 279 beds. By 2006, at $55 a day, the number of women in state custody had risen to 780. County jails were overflowing as bulldozers cleared sagebrush to make room for the South Boise Women's Correctional Center, another 160 beds. By 2013, Idaho was second only to Oklahoma in growth rate for female inmates. But women remained only 14 percent of Idaho's incarcerated. Smaller numbers meant fewer vocational programs, fewer inmate jobs, fewer law books, fewer facilities for those with mental illness, and fewer placements close to family and friends.

"Women are supposed to grin and bear it," said Taylar Nuevelle, an inmate and justice reporter. "Pap smears don't happen, mammograms go incomplete, and rape goes unreported."

Because male scholars prefer to write about men, and also perhaps because men have all but monopolized the most sensationally gruesome of violent crimes, Americans know shockingly little about the plight of women in prison. But historic places tell powerful stories. The Old Idaho Penitentiary is now a gold-star tourist attraction and national historic landmark. Its women's cellblock remains one of the nation's most visited and best preserved. Each year about 70,000 visitors take in the ward and its parent castlelike prison complex. Nearly 6,000 of these visitors are schoolchildren on educational tours.

"Touring the penitentiary fits in beautifully with the history class," says Dick Newton of Boise, a fourth-grade teacher. "The kids start their tour laughing and joking. But by the time they've finished, their mood is quite the reverse. It makes a lasting impression. It makes the young people think."

For staff, the interpretive challenge is to exhibit in thoughtful ways without whitewashing troublesome lives. It is an art, the curators say, of communicating complex ideas in simple and accessible language, of commenting on social justice without subordinating the past to the present, of stepping far enough back from physical objects to appreciate how history's pieces relate to the whole.

That task can be daunting with children. "What did *she* do?" asked a 10-year-old girl, pointing at the photo of a notorious inmate.

"She made a horrible decision," said the guide. "She harmed her children and ex-husband. They died. She is the only woman in Idaho who has ever been on death row."

The children gasped. Eyes bulged.

Who, what, and why are the threads we historians use to weave this volume of Idaho essays. A collective biography of 216 inmates, it is a book that looks bottom-up from the vantage of impoverished people, a story from an epoch in which female felons were baffling and rare. Chapters comment on murder and mayhem, chastity and prostitution, morphine and alcoholism, carjackings and stickups, petty cons with borrowed checkbooks, brawls, battery, a flypaper serial killer and the hacksaw she used to escape. More than 400 historical photos from the state's archival collection tell a parallel visual story. Mugshots frame colorless faces as truthfully as the past will allow.

Entry gate to the Women's Ward exhibit, 2020.
SOURCE: ISHS

Todd Shallat, PhD, is professor emeritus at Boise State University and the award-winning author of books and essays about cities and the environment.

Amber Beierle, MA, administers the Old Idaho Penitentiary and other sites for the Idaho State Historical Society.

The Old Idaho Penitentiary housed some of the Old West's most desperate outlaws. Opened in 1872, the prison complex held nearly 14,000 inmates. The site imprisoned only 216 women, mostly confined to a sandstone block house outside the main prison's northern wall. Antiquated conditions, overcrowding, and inmate uprisings closed the complex in 1973. Listed on the National Register of Historic Places, the "Old Pen" includes over 30 structures in the shadow of Boise's Table Rock. Over 70,000 people participate annually in guided and self-guided tours through cellblock exhibits, the gallows, and solitary confinement.

Taylor Thomas tours schoolchildren though the Old Idaho Penitentiary's No. 2 Cell House, 2018.
SOURCE: ISHS

The Old Idaho Penitentiary, a functioning prison from 1872 to 1973.
SOURCE: ISHS

Historian Anthony Parry, center, leads a penitentiary tour.
SOURCE: ISHS

Idaho's gender divide left women prisoners isolated with little supervision and very little to do. Pictured: Idaho's Women's Ward, built in 1906, modernized in 1920, now a free-standing cellblock in a world-class historic site.

SOURCE: ISHS

1950-1968

"The facilities for...women are strictly bad."

2

Murder and Mayhem

Judges and juries showed mercy to women who fought dangerous men.

By Todd Shallat and the Old Idaho Penitentiary staff

In Idaho, predatory murders of extreme violence were among the rarest of female crimes. From 1887 to 1968, before mass incarceration, when prison was the end of the road for only the most troublesome women, only one Idaho woman served time for murder in the first degree. None, so far, have been executed. Not even mothers who killed their children. Not even serial killers.

"It would seem, superficially at least, that if there is gender discrimination, it favors women," said criminologist Elizabeth Rapaport, crunching U.S. data from the 1970s and 1980s. Or so it had seemed to Rapaport before she probed the backstory of murder's gender divide. Women, if convicted with men, she found, were seldom the dominate aggressor. Few had slain women or children. Few had killed more than once. Most had killed in a rage or during a brawl or otherwise without plotted premeditation. Many had killed aggressively abusive men.

Crimes of violence committed by women, in short, were deemed by U.S. juries to be less diabolically savage than those committed by men. That was Idaho's story. Its first and third female penitentiary inmates, both killers of husbands, were a Shoshone-Bannock Indian named Henebe and a ranch wife named Josie Kensler. Both appear to have suffered beatings at the hands of their victims. Idaho's second female inmate, the suicidal and violent Margaret Hardy, was likewise a killer. Unlike most of the men sent to the Idaho State Penitentiary for murder, Hardy was too deranged to be isolated and too psychotic to understand the consequences of her crime.

Although self-defense was hard to establish, as were the lines between manslaughter and murder, welts and wounds and bludgeonings were tragically common. Phedora Crawford, for example, was a French immigrant who had survived a murderous melee in the Lemhi County gold camps. In 1898, Crawford sat for trial with two front teeth missing. Another battered woman who killed was the second-degree murderer Alwilda Reems, who, it seemed, had been raped and punched by her father, who was also her victim. A third was first-degree murderer Elizabeth Lacey, who, said the court, had spiked her husband's whiskey with strychnine. Lacey grimaced for her 1949 prison mugshot, posing in an open collar with a long white scar said to be courtesy of her spouse's attempt to slit open her throat with a knife.

In total, during eight decades of sandstone incarceration at the Idaho State Penitentiary, 51 women served 114 years for murder, manslaughter, and assault with a deadly weapon. Three out of five had prison files that noted abuse by a father or spouse.

Left: The hangman's noose was Idaho's final solution for 10 penitentiary convicts, 1878-1957. All were men. The state has yet to execute a woman.
SOURCE: ISHS

> **Fifty-one women served a total of 114 years for murder, manslaughter, and assault with a deadly weapon.**

Elizabeth Lacey dosed whiskey with strychnine, killing her abusive husband in 1949.
SOURCE: ISHS

Saloons and hotels crowd Boise's Main Street, looking south down 8th Street, 1907.

SOURCE: LIBRARY OF CONGRESS

Alta McGee fired into a crowd from a carriage in one of Boise's first drive-by shootings. Police seized the smoking pistol (right), a black steel Colt .38.

SOURCE: ISHS

A Woman Betrayed

Sometimes the abuse was psychological. Sometimes, in a society where jobs for women were few and economic dependence on men a reality, juries had sympathy, even admiration, for a woman with a whip or revolver who stood up to a philandering brute.

Boise's Alta McGee, age 36, was stout and bold and refused to roll over. In 1908, provoked by her husband, she loaded a pistol, rented a carriage, found the man outside a bar on Main Street, and fired wildly as he lounged in a crowd.

It may have been the capital city's first drive-by shooting, albeit via horse and buggy.

McGee's birth name and birthdate no longer survive in the public record. She may have been born in 1871 in Nebraska. First married in Chicago, she gave birth to a son, then divorced, then left for Montana. In 1905, perhaps in Nevada, she married a transient Irishman named John McGee, a bartender. A daughter was born. By 1907, with children in tow, the McGees had resettled in Boise. Police blotters picked up their trail on Main Street, where the couple rented a house and the husband tangled with patrons

of the back-alley bawdy district. More than once, reported the *Idaho Statesman*, the ne'er-do-well cheat McGee had taunted his wife by driving past the family's home in an open carriage with a painted girlfriend. The wife, enraged, had once pulled John's suitor from the passenger seat of the carriage and horsewhipped the girl in the street.

On the evening of May 4, 1908, with a black .38 in her lap, Alta and a female friend rode in a rented carriage searching the back-alley district for John. They found him at about 10 p.m. outside the Pioneer Saloon on Main Street. Rising from the carriage, Alta fired. Two bullets hit brick. A third shattered a gaslit cigar store window where Boise City Hall now stands.

"I shot at my husband. I don't know if I hit him or not," Alta McGee exclaimed, flustered in the hands of police.

On September 23, after an 18-hour jury deliberation, charges of attempted murder were reduced to assault with a deadly weapon. Sympathizers were many and of the outspoken opinion that the womanizer had gotten pretty much what he deserved. The wife, after all, had been scorned. Clemency came on Christmas Day, 1908, when Governor Frank R. Gooding emptied the women's cellblock, releasing McGee, Kensler, and two other inmates. Alta McGee's total time in the women's cellblock was 65 days.

"Flypaper Lyda"

Even Idaho's most notorious inmate — a woman who had killed her kin for money without a wince of remorse — was spared the noose by a male jury. One juror simply refused to allow a woman to be executed no matter what she had done.

Lyda Southard, aka Idaho's Lady Bluebeard, was named Ann Eliza Trueblood at birth. Born in 1892 in rural Missouri, she was the second of 11 children and impoverished after the father died. Southard later spoke of the heartbreak of having to sell her pet milk cows to feed the family. Years later, in prison, she would dribble out crumbs to the wild birds that danced between the iron bars set into concrete. One bird she named Sylvia. Feral cats often were dumped near the ward, and Southard tamed the wildest of them.

The murders may have started soon after Southard's marriage to a strapping young farmer named Robert Dooley, the first of seven husbands. The couple soon had a daughter they named Lorraine. Southard, as became her murderous pattern, insisted that Dooley buy life insurance. Soon the husband, a brother-in-law, and an infant daughter were dead from what appeared to be typhoid fever, perhaps contracted from the farm's dirty well, the widow said. The year was 1915. Southard claimed the insurance money and sold her dead husband's farm.

Always, with Southard, it was about the life insurance. Husband number two, a homesteader, lasted only 18 months before succumbing to what appeared to be diphtheria or the flu. Husband number three soon died with similar symptoms after three months of marriage. Medical examiners initially blamed the death on "complications [from] gastroenteritis." Later it was alleged that the victims had been poisoned with arsenic. Extracted from drugstore flypaper, the poison may have been brewed into lemonade and baked into apple pies.

Husband number four, a Twin Falls ranch foreman, died groaning in a hospital ward. Later at trial a hospital nurse would recall that the widow had given the dying husband mysterious glasses of water. Again, the cause of death appeared to be gastroenteritis or typhoid.

Lyda Southard, convicted in 1921, was imprisoned longer than any other female inmate, serving nearly 20 years.
SOURCE: ISHS

Birds, feral cats, and men with insurance gravitated toward Lady Bluebeard (Lyda Southard).

POISON

Flypaper was a common killer of husbands before laws restricted the sale of arsenic insecticides. Boiled flypaper from the killer's kitchen helped to convict Lyda Southard at trial.

Right: Lyda Southard poses between her captors, Deputy Sheriff Virgil "Val" Ormsby, left, and Sheriff E.R. Sherman, 1921.

By 1919, at age 27, Southard had amassed nearly $10,000 (equivalent to perhaps $260,000 in 2020). People were getting suspicious. Under an alias, she fled to Los Angeles, where husband number five was a petty officer in the U.S. Navy. The newlyweds set sail for the naval base at Pearl Harbor, Hawaii.

Back in Twin Falls, meanwhile, a district attorney was up for reelection, voters were asking questions, and the sheriff had started to wonder how a widow so rich could be so unlucky. Virgil "Val" Ormsby, the county's deputy sheriff, was assigned to the case. A clever investigator, he used forensic tools that were quite advanced for the day. Corpses were exhumed from graves as distant as Sandpoint. Forensic experts found traces of arsenic in pots and pans from Southard's ranch house kitchen. Southard, tracked down in Honolulu, was arrested and returned to Twin Falls.

"She swept the men of her choice off their feet," reported a Philadelphia newspaper. She was a "black widow," a "temptress." With lethal smiles "she had courted [men] so persistently that they could not escape."

By October 1921, standing room only in the brass and mahogany Twin Falls County courthouse, Deputy Ormsby had narrowed the prosecutorial focus to the unfortunate Edward Meyer — one of five, possibly six, who may have ingested arsenic. The deceptive killing effect of the poison became key to the case.

For centuries the pale liquid crystallized metal had been the toxin of choice for would-be assassins of famous people such as Napoleon and Great Britain's George III. Tasteless, hard to trace, easy to acquire, arsenic mimicked the sudden blue-choking fevered death of people with WWI influenza and other rampant diseases.

Southard pled "not guilty" even as the evidence mounted. A hardware clerk recalled that the woman had made an unusual purchase of nine sheets of arsenic flypaper. A ranch cook found flypaper sheets in a bedroom Southard had briefly shared with her spouse. A doctor on the stand conceded that the deceased foreman had symptoms not inconsistent with poisoning by flypaper arsenic. Through it all, sitting without emotion and dressed to the nines —

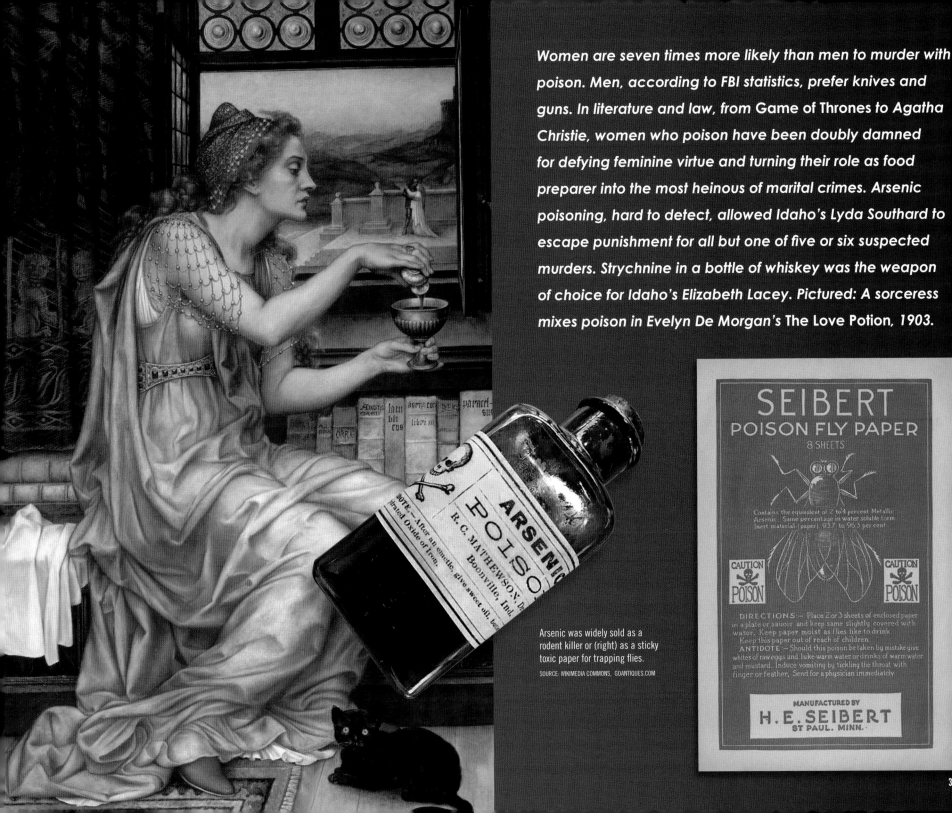

Women are seven times more likely than men to murder with poison. Men, according to FBI statistics, prefer knives and guns. In literature and law, from Game of Thrones to Agatha Christie, women who poison have been doubly damned for defying feminine virtue and turning their role as food preparer into the most heinous of marital crimes. Arsenic poisoning, hard to detect, allowed Idaho's Lyda Southard to escape punishment for all but one of five or six suspected murders. Strychnine in a bottle of whiskey was the weapon of choice for Idaho's Elizabeth Lacey. Pictured: A sorceress mixes poison in Evelyn De Morgan's The Love Potion, 1903.

Arsenic was widely sold as a rodent killer or (right) as a sticky toxic paper for trapping flies.

SOURCE: WIKIMEDIA COMMONS, GOANTIQUES.COM

3

Right: Lyda Southard's all-male jury, Twin Falls County Courthouse, 1921.

SOURCE: ISHS

LYDA SOUTHARD . . . married 'em and buried 'em.

"I'll bake you up a bunch of biscuits," said Lyda Southard to her jailers, having killed at least one husband with arsenic in an apple pie.

SOURCE: ISHS

tan suit with mink trim, silk stockings, French heeled pumps — the defendant seemed heartless.

On Monday, November 6 , 1921, the five-week trial ended with a jury deliberation of 23 hours. Because the charge was murder in the first degree, and because that capital crime was likely to trigger the death penalty, one anonymous male juror held out for full acquittal. The negotiated compromise was second-degree murder with a penitentiary sentence of 10 years to life. Two days later the judge gaveled the verdict. Southard, smiling coolly and not waiting for her lawyer's appeal, was escorted by car to Boise for mugshots and fingerprinting.

"Gracious, I don't know how long it will take," said Southard of the appeal. "I thought I might as well begin my sentence now [instead of] sticking in the Twin Falls jail."

Newsworthy sightings in the years to follow placed the celebrity widow outside the prison in the company of matrons and escorts. Two years into her sentence a rumor of her pregnancy had so humiliated a prison official that he went public to denounce it as a "damnable outrage." But serious mischief was brewing. Southard had managed to get prison trustees and cons to help her construct a garden lattice. Made from old pipes, it could be scaled like a tall thin ladder. David Minton — a suitor, a former inmate — may have provided the widow with the blade of a hacksaw. A rope braided from blankets was also used.

The escape came in the Boise moonlight on May 4, 1931. An illustration in the *Salt Lake Tribune* pictured the widow dangling from a rope like a Hollywood femme fatale, swinging into the arms of a waiting accomplice. Minton, the con, who played the sap in media drama, had outfitted a roadster with camping equipment. The fugitives, it was said, fled east, leaving a trail of speculation. One rumor had them on a plane to Mexico. Another had them tented in a Canadian forest. Or maybe,

$500-00 $500-00

$50⁰⁰ REWARD $50⁰⁰

MRS. LYDA SOUTHARD, No. 3052

...entiary, Boise, Idaho, on the night of May 4th, 1931. ...1921, from Twin Falls County. Charge: ... 142 pounds;

rumor had it, Southard had ditched Minton and had slow-freighted to China.

But Southard, in fact, was under the cover of a new alias in Denver. She had found work as a housekeeper for the sick wife and young son of a man named Harry Whitlock. When Whitlock's wife died, predictably, Southard and Whitlock wed.

"He has a pleasing personality and was very good to me," said Southard of husband number six.

In the spring of 1932, as the law kept searching for Southard, a reward poster offering $50 piqued the interest of Minton, the jilted accomplice. The former con, himself a fugitive, tipped the authorities that the widow might have remarried in Denver. But Southard, a step ahead, had already slipped into Kansas. Police found her posting mail in Topeka. Husband Whitlock pocketed the $50 and filed for divorce. Southard returned to the Women's Ward at the Idaho State Penitentiary.

An uneventful decade of card-playing and radio music followed in the lonely cellblock in the shadow of men with rifles on turreted walls. Southard in loose-fitting gingham began showing matronly weight and was no longer invited to the parks for picnics. At last in 1941, after 18 years, 7 months, and 23 days, which was more time spent in the ward than any other female convict, Southard won the governor's conditional pardon. The condition was that she live with a sister and not sell her story. Full pardon came in 1943 at age 51. "Drop around to see me . . . boys," she said, winking at her Idaho jailers when she left prison, "and I'll bake you a bunch of biscuits." Death

by heart attack struck her without warning 15 years later on a city street in Salt Lake City, Utah.

Southard, by then, was nationally infamous. Pulp exposés with lurid covers called her Idaho's "Lady Bluebeard," a reference to the French folktale in which a bearded nobleman kills many wives. *Time* magazine, in 1941, called her "Flypaper Lyda." A 1994 biography advanced the dubious claim that the housewife from Twin Falls had been America's first serial killer.

Radio music and card-playing broke the boredom in the women's cellblock during the era of Lyda Southard.

Left: Satanic voices haunt Idaho's arsenic widow in this 1942 issue of *The American Weekly*, calling her "fatally charming."

SOURCE: ISHS

Margaret Barney (top) and Verna Keller escaped over the wall on a lark with the help of a makeshift ladder, 1948.

SOURCE: ISHS

The call came in from Payette. Keller and Barney, for a night, had escaped.

Tarzan Escapes

The call came in collect from the lumber town of Payette. On the morning of April 7, 1948, Warden Louis E. Clapp had just sat down for breakfast when the phone rang in his office. Send a car, said the caller. Two inmates had escaped 12 hours earlier.

The escape took a bit of planning. Cellmates Verna "Tarzan" Keller, age 17, and Margaret M. Barney, age 21, loosened an iron bar from the concrete slab at the base of their window. Using timbers from a coal bin and finding nails, they fashioned a makeshift ladder. Atop the wall they crouched in the dark while a watchman rounded a corner. Jumping and scrambling through sagebrush, they made their way to Old Route 30, hitching rides through town toward the Oregon border.

"You girls thought we were kidding but we had it all planned," read the note Keller had left in her cell. "I am going to see my mother. We will be back soon." Warden Clapp shrugged. The two had escaped on a lark, it seemed, just to prove that they could do it. He called it a prank by two bored inmates desperate for a night on the town.

Crimes more vicious than pranks had sent Keller to the Women's Ward. Born in Montana, she was one of eight children in a family searching for work in the North Idaho town of Sandpoint. By age 14 Keller was known to police as a habitual truant, drinking with men, running away from home. One arrest truancy had landed the teenager in the girls' industrial reformatory school in St. Anthony. Returned to Sandpoint to attend the 10th grade,

Keller subsequently dropped out, married a teenager, annulled the marriage, remarried, divorced, and then was charged by Oregon police with lewd cohabitation.

Keller's capital crime, overtly sexual and shockingly violent, occurred in a Sandpoint alley on a winter's night in 1947. Intoxicated, Keller and the man she lived with, Roscoe Hartley, stalked a 16-year-old girl named Juanita Plaster. Keller may have thought the younger girl was flirting with Hartley. Lured into the alley, the girl took a blow to the skull. Keller and Hartley then tore off the victim's slacks and beat her to death barehanded. The girl's underwear was stuffed in her mouth to silence her dying moans.

Convicted with Hartley in Bonner County, Keller pled down to murder in the second degree. "Everything went so fast," Keller confessed at trial. "I didn't realize I had hit her so hard."

Doubly Victimized

Keller and Southard were Idaho exceptions to the American rule about 20th-century women in jail or prison for murder. Nationwide, historically, very few women had killed other women.

A recent fact sheet from Tennessee's Family Safety Center estimated that 9 out of 10 women currently imprisoned for murder had been raped or beaten by the man they later killed. In 1987, in one of the first data-driven studies, author and forensic psychologist Charles Patrick Ewing reported that as many as 1,000 women a year are sent to prison for slaying an attacking husband or boyfriend. "This small but increasingly visible minority," said Ewing, "[were] doubly victimized — first by their male attacker, then by a system of criminal justice which holds [women] to an unrealistic standard of accountability."

Idaho's Women Ward data confirm that tragic pattern. Before the era of mass incarceration, in a state where fiscal pragmatism seems to have been the overriding principle of jurisprudence, there were 27 female manslaughter cases. Eleven had domestic violence noted in criminal files. Convicted survivors, they were women who had been slashed by razors (Mary Turner Hansom, Phyllis Miller, Lucille Haram), assaulted in bedrooms (Mary Barnes, Jeannette Benoy), or were diving and scrambling for guns at the time the crime was committed (Doris Anstine, Josephine Fort, Virginia Mahoney).

There appears to have been no clear sentencing standard. In 1936, for example, Luella Yates of Jerome stood in her yard with a shotgun leveled at a quarrelsome neighbor. The man, advancing, was fuming about wandering cattle. A blast of buckshot intended for the dirt clipped the man's knee. Later in the hospital he died from a blood infection. Townspeople pled for mercy. Hundreds signed a petition. In court, murder in the second degree was changed to involuntary

Idaho Girls Reformatory in St. Anthony.
SOURCE: ISHS

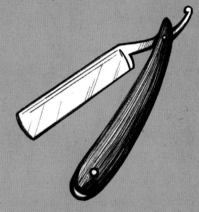

Razor cuts, recorded by prison officials, were the marks of horrific abuse.

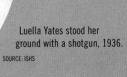

Luella Yates stood her ground with a shotgun, 1936.
SOURCE: ISHS

39

The case of Doris Anstine, who killed her husband in 1965, reached the Idaho Supreme Court in a dispute over a murderer's rightful claim to marital property rights.

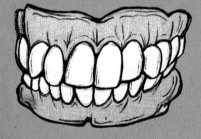

A brawl left Anstine in bruises. Anstine's husband struck her so hard the dentures flew from her face.

her husband began to berate and abuse her. He grabbed a loaded rifle and threatened her with it. She pled with him to lay down the weapon. Tossing it on the bed, he hit her barehanded, striking her so hard her dentures flew from her mouth. She lunged for the rifle. It fired. A bullet struck the man in the chest.

"Doris, you've hurt me," wheezed her husband, bleeding out before medical help arrived.

Attorneys in the subsequent trial long debated whether the shooting was premeditated or accidental. Another question was whether the widow, having killed, should inherit the home. It took 18 months for the Idaho Supreme Court to uphold the lower court's verdict of voluntary manslaughter. Sentenced in 1966, Anstine walked free after a year and eight months, on the day that Idaho forever shuttered the Women's Ward at the Idaho State Penitentiary.

Some women got away with murder. Some got away with nothing, battered by cycles of violence, having little control over their lives.

manslaughter with a minimum two-year sentence. Clemency by way of the governor's pardon came to Yates after a year and two months.

A final case of a woman who killed a belligerent battering spouse was one of the last to spend time in the Women's Ward. Doris Anstine, age 41, was a tavern worker in Kootenai County. Standing just 4 feet 10 inches with cropped hair, her prison mugshot reveals a sad face with a broken spirit. Decades earlier, as a girl in Payette, she had fled her father's home to escape the man's abuse and alcoholism. Three bad marriages followed. On January 15, 1965, Doris and her third husband, Elmer, were drinking together at a bar in Rathdrum. Upon returning home,

Todd Shallat, PhD, scripted this chapter from research provided by Skye Cranney and staff associates at the Old Idaho Penitentiary.

State of Crime

Women Inmates by County, 1887-1968

12+ Inmates

9-11 Inmates

4-8 Inmates

1-3 Inmates

Some inmates were incarcerated multiple times; each instance is included in the total. *Inmate #3417 was a federal prisoner and is included in Ada County.

BOUNDARY 1

BONNER 4

KOOTENAI 11

BENEWAH

SHOSHONE 6

LATAH 4

CLEARWATER 5

NEZ PERCE 31

LEWIS 2

IDAHO 1

LEMHI 4

ADAMS

VALLEY 1

CUSTER

CLARK

FREEMONT

WASHINGTON 4

PAYETTE 1

GEM 4

BOISE

JEFFERSON 2

MADISON 3

TETON

BUTTE

CANYON 10

ADA 30

ELMORE 3

CAMAS

BLAINE 1

BONNEVILLE 8

BINGHAM 12

GOODING

LINCOLN 2

POWER 1

CARIBOU 1

OWYHEE 2

TWIN FALLS 25

JEROME 6

MINIDOKA 3

BANNOCK 25

CASSIA 8

ONEIDA

FRANKLIN

BEAR LAKE

PHOTO SOURCE: ROYCE WILLIAMS

Prisoners at Boise's Table Rock mesa began breaking stone for public buildings in the decade of Idaho statehood. Convict labor cut stone for the penitentiary's wall and administration building, completed in 1894. Pictured: A crane hoists stone from the mesa's quarry, about 1905.

Unrighteous Wrongs

Severe penalties for "moral" offenses punished women abandoned by men.

By Karen Benning

"In her present condition," wrote a prosecuting attorney about 19-year-old Mary Mills, "I regard her as a menace to society." It sounds harsh now, but in 1936 when these words were written, the attorney had only three categories from which to choose about the girl: "menace to society," "habitual criminal," or someone "who has made a mistake." Not among the options: confused adolescent. Still-grieving daughter. Victim of those who were older and savvier. All of these or none of these might be true, but there will never be any way to know. When it comes to Mary Mills, there are more questions than answers about why she turned 20 years old in prison.

A few years earlier, the Mills family was living in the small town of Gooding, Idaho, where Mary's father worked as a store clerk. It was the day after Christmas when Werden Mills suddenly had a cerebral hemorrhage; before the day was out, he was dead. He was just 42 years old, and his only daughter had turned 16 three months before. The country was three years into the Great Depression, and Mary's mother, Verdia, had not only the girl but her 12-year-old brother to feed. What happened next remains unclear, although turning out one's own children was not unheard of during the Depression. What we do know is that almost exactly three years after her father died, Mary stood unsmiling before a camera, a butterfly-shaped clip in her hair and the oversized numbers "5 2 3 1" on a placard spanning her chest. It was three days after Christmas, 1935.

Women Detached

In the first half of the 20th century, what was a mother to do if her husband died and they had already been poor to begin with? Although not always the case, many "morality crimes" leading to the imprisonment of women at the Idaho State Penitentiary were either directly or indirectly related to the absence of a man, who would have much more easily been able to access economic opportunities. Convictions related to morality might involve the distribution or even home use of alcohol through the many years of Prohibition, or they could relate to exposing another person to a "dangerous disease," which, based on specific cases, appears to have been a euphemism for sexually transmitted disease. (Nobody was ever convicted for coughing on someone and giving them the flu, for example.) But the most common morality crime for which women were sent to the Women's Ward of the Idaho State Penitentiary in the early 20th century was not the breaking of Prohibition laws, or spreading disease, and, surprisingly, not even prostitution. It was adultery.

For women on their own, the options were few, even well before the Great Depression. But death wasn't the only way a woman could find herself without her husband (or a girl without her father), who was often her only means of financial support.

Divorce rates soared and marriages crashed during the Great Depression as young men took to the highways and young mothers were left to fend for themselves.

SOURCE: LIBRARY OF CONGRESS

Left: Syphilitic skull, 1910. Sexually transmitted diseases inflamed the Progressive crusade against adultery and prostitution.

SOURCE: NATIONAL MUSEUM OF HEALTH AND MEDICINE

One in five turn-of-the-century workers were minors under the age of 16. Hattie McCormick (née Blank) worked as a laborer and domestic servant after being turned out of her house at age 9. Pictured: A sister and brother, ages 12 and 8, work in a mill for six cents an hour, 1908.

SOURCE: CHILD LABOR COMMITTEE

Such severance could come about with a shocking swiftness. Childhood was no protection, as Hattie McCormick (née Blank) found out when she was about 9 years old. Within a year of her mother's death during childbirth, Hattie had been turned out of her home. It is not clear where she went to live or how she survived the remainder of her childhood and then adolescence. But during those years, in the 1880s and 1890s, a child on her own would have warranted little notice, much less any kind of nurturing intervention. A more likely response might have been, "Why aren't you working?" accompanied by a brief reprimand. After all, children had plenty of opportunities to "pull themselves up by their own bootstraps." Child labor laws would not appear for another 50 years.

When Hattie Blank was a child, her peers throughout the country were often put to work on farms, in stores, in mills, and in mines and factories. They hawked newspapers and worked as messengers and shined shoes. They served as apprentices in the trades. As one article notes, well into the 20th century, "the arrival of a newborn to a rural family was viewed by the parents as a future beneficial laborer." If, for whatever reason, a household found itself out of balance in its supply of children versus its need for help around the house or on the property, the family "would often send children to another household that could employ them as a maid, servant, or plowboy." When Hattie was growing up in the 1880s and 1890s, approximately one in every five children worked.

For obvious reasons, those who employed children weren't necessarily supportive of compulsory education. Hattie would only move from Oregon, where she was born, to Idaho in her late 20s, but the picture of compulsory education was fairly similar across the country. It was shortly after Hattie's mother had died, and right around the time the girl left home, that Idaho passed the Compulsory Education Act of 1887, which applied to children ages 8 to 14. However, the law was passed by the Territorial Legislature, since Idaho's statehood lay three years in the future. And, as in most parts of the country where compulsory education laws were being enacted, enforcement was another matter entirely. Many decades would pass before compulsory education would overtake the prevalence of child labor.

It is not clear whether Hattie was sent someplace where she would receive any kind of education; the most likely scenario is that she was left to find her own way and ended up working for a family somewhere near her home community in eastern Oregon.

Since her father was still alive, Hattie was not an orphan, but had she been, her situation might not have drawn any greater sympathy. One U.S. orphanage epitomized a prevailing attitude throughout the country when it decided to provide

"A" stood for adultery in the scarlet letter worn by a Puritan woman in Nathaniel Hawthorne's historical novel about morality, guilt, and lust. Left: Jesus shows mercy to a remorseful woman in Guercino's *The Woman Taken in Adultery*, about 1621.

SOURCE: WIKIMEDIA COMMONS

Adultery and lust pervaded the Bible verses that were the foundation of morality laws.

nothing to its young charges for free, but to treat them as "independent little dealers and give them nothing without payment" in order to avoid "the growth of a future dependent class." Opponents of public benefits echo that same phrase today.

But Hattie Blank, who would become Hattie McCormick at the age of 16 and proceed to give birth to a total of eight children in her lifetime, did not land in Idaho's penitentiary for any crime one might suppose based on her troubling early years — thievery, say, or maybe prostitution or writing bad checks. Instead, she spent a little over four months in the state prison for adultery. She served time for adultery even though by the time of her arrest in 1909, when she was not quite 30 years old, she and her first husband had separated. She had left Oregon to live near her father, who had moved to Pine Creek, Idaho, between current-day Coeur d'Alene and Wallace. (That move in itself raises even more questions than answers about her father's actions when his daughter was just 9 years old.) When she met William Hasten Goodman, a local man 15 years her senior, he told her that he, too, was separated.

It is not clear who made the complaint, but the two were arrested and convicted. Separation wasn't enough; you had to be officially divorced before carrying on with a new partner. Though Hattie was sentenced to a year in the penitentiary for adultery, she was released early under several conditions, none of which included that she refrain from the crime of which she had been convicted. Instead, she had to agree to avoid alcohol, tobacco, and gambling, none of which are mentioned as factors in her original

arrest. Her crime may have been questionable, but her punishments were all but nonsensical.

Morality and Class

Mary Beattie (née Neibaur) was 16 years old when she first married in 1915. She moved in with her new husband, William Beattie, on his family's farm near Rexburg, Idaho. In addition to the three children she bore him, he already had an infant daughter, indicating his first wife may have died while giving birth or shortly thereafter. Her stepdaughter was 6 and the other three were infants or toddlers when William was imprisoned for the sexual assault of a 14-year-old girl.

Accounts vary, but 1920 census records indicate that Mary's parents, Hyrum and Alice Neibaur, were renting a home in Sugar City at the time of their daughter's marriage and that Mary's father, Hyrum, worked as a laborer in the local sugar factory. They apparently moved to Rexburg with their three youngest children, perhaps so that Alice and Mary could help each other with the care and feeding of the combined brood — two adolescents and five who were still under

Bedding men out of wedlock sent at least 10 women to state prison during Idaho's first 100 years.

Right: Mary Beattie and her mother Alice Neibaur had been caring for seven children when police found them in amorous congress with men who were not their husbands.
SOURCE: ISHS

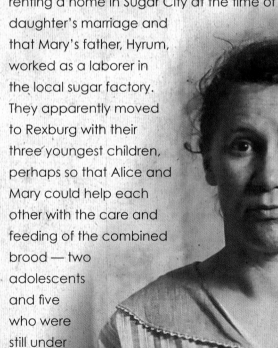

age 8. At this point Hyrum found work as a miner, but not for long.

Among the children was Mary's stepdaughter, who was 7 when Hyrum was arrested the following year for sexually assaulting (assault with intent to rape) another girl of the same age. It was his third arrest for the same type of crime. Now mother and daughter both had a husband in the Idaho State Penitentiary, both for the sexual assault of underage girls.

Who tipped off the police? It could have been William's father, who still owned the farm and may have resented the mass intrusion of someone else's family while his own son sat in the penitentiary. Not only that, he had a solid reputation in town, and the Neibaurs were considered "low class" by other members of his community. To add insult to injury, not just his daughter-in-law but also her mother were both up to no good with other men.

It was three in the morning when the local sheriff and another police officer raided the farm in Rexburg. They found Mrs. Beattie in bed with a man named

David Evans, who worked at the sugar factory back in Sugar City. Her mother, 50-year-old Alice Neibaur, was also in bed with a man not her husband — a 42-year-old sheepherder named Mike O'Rourke, who had "been known to have associated with other low class women in a similar way." Alice, too, had a reputation that would not help: "It has been known to officers of this County that the prisoner has been leading an immoral life for [a] considerable length of time."

Alice Neibaur's penitentiary intake form included that she was raised in the Mormon church. That she attended Sunday school. That she had seven years of formal education and could read and write. That she had "very bad" teeth but no beard. ("N/A" had not come into use yet.) That her mother died when she was 8 years old. And that, when asked what he thought her "criminal tendencies" were, the prosecuting attorney asserted that Alice was "a moral degenerate." Her daughter, too, could read and write although she only had a fifth-grade education. That her teeth were not quite as bad as her mother's but probably soon would be. Neither

Most of the Women's Ward inmates were mothers. At least 10 entered the ward while pregnant. Today nationwide, of the 2.8 million women imprisoned each year, 80 percent are mothers.

Adultery, Religion, and Law

The U.S. Supreme Court, in *Lemon v. Kurtzman* (1971), struck down "an excessive government entanglement with religion" at the foundation of morality legislation. Eight states still defended a secular right to protect traditional marriage, leaving, by the 1990s, a nationwide patchwork of laws. Map: Status of adultery laws, 1996.

- NO STATUTE
- GROUNDS FOR DIVORCE ONLY
- CRIMINALIZES SEX OUTSIDE OF MARRIAGE, MISDEMEANOR
- ILLEGAL ONLY IF ADULTEROUS COUPLE COHABITS, MISDEMEANOR
- CRIMINALIZES SEX OUTSIDE OF MARRIAGE, FELONY
- ADULTERY CONVICTION AFFECTS SPOUSAL PROPERTY RIGHTS ONLY

Right: Cyrena Thompson lost her husband to the 1918 flu pandemic. Charged with adultery and neglecting her children, she served seven months of a three-year sentence.

SOURCE: ISHS

woman had ever had a criminal charge before. And now they, as well as both men who had been found with them, were convicted of adultery. A mother and daughter, both of their husbands, and both of their lovers all ended up at the state penitentiary at the same time. The children were shipped off to the Children's Home in Boise, with the exception of Mary's 3-year-old son Kenneth, who was sent to the Nampa School, an institution for "epileptics and the feeble minded."

For Cyrena Thompson (née Young), who went by her middle name "Irene," it was a death followed by a man's deception that landed her in the penitentiary for adultery. Married at 15 and with a fifth-grade education, she had six children by the time her husband died at the end of 1918, a victim of the influenza ("Spanish flu") pandemic. The family had moved to Burley, Idaho, earlier that year; born in Utah, Thompson was left on her own, likely with no nearby family support. Within a few years she had been charged twice with neglect of her children, who were sent to the Boise Children's Home. Then she met Benjamin Summers, who told her he was separated from his wife. He gave her a place to live. (He also likely gave her a sexually transmitted disease.)

One of Summers's own six children, an 18-year-old daughter, had been arrested for "illicit cohabitation." Whether for a lighter sentence or out of sheer spite, she volunteered that her father was also illicitly cohabitating with a woman not his wife. Summers

50

Prostitution was no longer politely dismissed as a necessary evil after President Howard Taft, in 1910, signed the White Slave Traffic Act. Called the Mann Act after its sponsor, the law made it a felony to cross state lines with a woman or girl for "debauchery" or any other "immoral purpose." Idaho's Edna Carlton was convicted under the act for transporting a prostitute from Mountain Home to Seattle. Pictured: Puck magazine damns "white slavery," 1915.

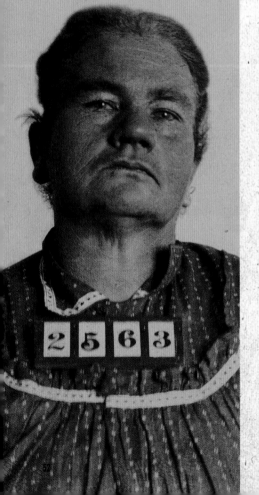

and Thompson were both arrested and sent to the penitentiary. Although Summers had lied to Thompson about his marital status, the prosecuting attorney in the case offered that Summers had potential. "Inherently he is not bad," he wrote. "He can make good and become an asset to society." Of Thompson he said that she was "probably not criminally inclined" but that she was weak, lacked morals, and had "made herself . . . wholly unfit for any use to herself or anyone else."

Today, adultery is still illegal in 21 states, although Idaho is just one of five states where it is considered a felony. As late as 1991, the issue could prove surprisingly divisive; efforts in one state to decriminalize adultery led to fears that it would lead to the entire state becoming a "moral wasteland." In Idaho, although the law is rarely enforced, committing adultery could lead to up to three years in prison and a fine of up to $1,000.

The last woman convicted of adultery and sentenced to the Women's Ward before it closed in 1968 was Leora Eliason, in 1942. Eliason, Thompson, and Neibaur each ultimately married the man with whom their affair had led to their imprisonment.

Cycles of Victimization

It's not hard to infer that Mary Beattie and perhaps her mother, Alice Neibaur, may both have been caught up in a generational cycle of victimhood by men with patterns of sexual assault and abuse, one of the many repercussions of women's societally enforced

financial dependence on men. It is also not hard to understand why some women turned to unlawful activities for money when so many lawful avenues were closed to them. Dora Harvill, however, is a more difficult case. She may have been a victim, a perpetrator, or both. It depends on how much credence one gives to hearsay — early 20th-century Idaho courts apparently gave it quite a lot.

Harvill was in her mid-40s when she and her husband of nearly 30 years divorced in 1914. Several years later she moved in with a boyfriend. With her was the last of her seven children, Edith, who was 12. What the police who raided the home witnessed was the boyfriend, named James Dugger, in bed with the girl. He was arrested on the spot, but so was Harvill, with the evidence of her complicity that she was in an adjoining room with "no door closed between the two rooms." Both Harvill and Dugger were convicted of rape and sent to the Idaho State Penitentiary; the difference in the views about them emerged later, after Harvill was released early, having served only 3½ years of her 10-year sentence, thanks to her advanced age (48) and another daughter's request for clemency. Dugger decided to try for similar treatment. The letters poured in from community members on his behalf, many placing the full blame on Harvill.

"After they went to Prison," wrote a police officer who had made the initial arrests, "I heard how this woman [Harvill] went about the country in a single buggy," peddling her daughter to men. Although there is no proof, it is possible that Dugger, who was younger than Harvill, presented himself as her boyfriend, offering shelter to the two in exchange for access to the child.

Dugger tried to make the case that at the worst, he should be treated as an adulterer rather than a rapist. His argument? "It is a well known fact that this girl . . . was committing adultery with other men long before I became acquainted with them." Neither the police officer nor Dugger offered any evidence to back up their accusations.

Dugger also appears to have believed that sexual relations with a 12-year-old were just fine due to her past. If the stories were true, then it is possible the girl's mother had been pimping her. That somehow also made the daughter at fault. "It was not a case of forceable (sic) rape," wrote one of the jurors, "it was legal — safe because of the age of the girl." (Although by 1920 the age of consent in Idaho had been raised to 18, in many states for many years it had been 10 to 12, and attitudes can be slower to change than laws.) The juror went on to explain that the child was "well developed and could pass for 18," and stated that the incident with Dugger had occurred with the girl's consent, as though she would have had any choice in the matter. At the time of the trial, the girl was several months pregnant.

Harvill's daughter was shipped off to the children's orphanage and reform school in eastern Idaho. A petition made the rounds demanding Dugger's early release from prison, and in July 1927 he received a pardon.

From the time Verna Shipley married a truck driver named Richard Byers in 1928 until they were both sent to the penitentiary nine years later, they had moved at least six times and lived in at least four different states, including Iowa, South Dakota, Montana, and Idaho, where they were both arrested for the same charge — exposing others to a venereal disease, namely, syphilis. It was Verna's first criminal charge, but Richard already had a record that included writing worthless checks and, in the era of Prohibition, liquor charges.

Two disturbing details offer clues as to the true nature of how syphilis was spread, at least among the Byerses. After their conviction, the prosecuting attorney recanted his accusation of Verna. "There was no intent on her part," he came to believe, "to deliberately expose another to venereal disease." Conspicuously, he made no such claim about her husband. Worse, at the time of their arrest, both of the

She may be.. a bag of TROUBLE SYPHILIS - GONORRHEA

Syphilis plagued Verna Byers and her trucker husband as they traveled through four western states. Left: Public hygiene poster warns against sexually transmitted diseases, 1940.

SOURCE: ISHS, WIKIMEDIA COMMONS

Moses Alexander knew a thing or two about controlling the criminal classes by banning the sale of booze. As Boise's mayor in 1901, he had allied with temperance crusaders to shut down the bawdy houses. As governor in 1916, he championed statewide prohibition. Helen Hall of Salmon and Hannah Folden of Sandpoint served penitentiary time for prohibition violations. Left: Boise office of the Woman's Christian Temperance Union, 1914; temperance poster, 1874.

children — Juanita, who would have been about 6 years old, and Teddy, about 4 — also had syphilis.

Verna and Richard Byers were given reprieve early and freed from prison after less than eight months. They left the state together after their release, their children back in their custody.

Prostitution

Related to spreading sexually transmitted disease is another type of offense that could be considered a morality crime — prostitution. However, prostitutes were often simply thrown into the local jail rather than sent to the state prison. If a community really wanted to rid themselves of a woman suspected of or charged with prostitution, there were other ways to get her sent off to the penitentiary. Often it involved finding other crimes with which to charge her. That was the case, for example, with Helen Hall. Attractive and wearing a flowered dress for her mugshot, in multiple records her eye color was noted as "orange." It may have been such a light brown as to appear amber, but perhaps that was too fine a nuanced hue for the bureaucrats processing her paperwork. So orange it was.

Hall had a reputation in her east-central Idaho community of Salmon for running a "house of ill fame." But that's not what she was arrested for.

It was an autumn day in 1932. A little over a year later, Prohibition would be repealed. When Hall was charged, the nationwide ban on alcohol had been in effect for well over a decade. But that's not what she was arrested for, either, or not exactly.

There was a young man in the community who at 19 was already "in the habit of drinking." No legal minimum drinking age existed because alcohol was supposed to be off-limits to all. Yet somehow the

Orange eyes meant debauchery to the prosecutors in Lemhi Country who accused Helen Hall of running what they called "a house of ill fame."
SOURCE: ISHS

young man had formed a drinking habit. While it is unlikely that Hall was the first or only person to supply him with drink, she was the one who was arrested for it. The reasoning? He had not yet reached the age of majority, which was 21. It was a business exchange;

the man had offered to clean off her car for payment in alcohol.

Although a girl could legally be married off well before that age, giving liquor to a 19-year-old male was enough to get Hall sent away to the Women's Ward at the Idaho State Penitentiary in Boise. She spent six months in prison for the charge of giving intoxicating liquors to a minor. This also afforded the courts the opportunity to label her a menace to society. Like a number of female inmates, upon her release she seems to have simply disappeared from any traceable records. Did she change her ways, become a respectable citizen, find a man to marry and take care of her? Or did she return to Salmon with the cloud of a conviction hanging over her head, her home confiscated by the City, and drift toward a bleak future?

Without a man to provide financial support in the era that the Women's Ward was in operation, two options women had were to either find a man (preferably one who wouldn't abuse them or their children), or to try and go it alone using whatever skills they could employ. Hall attempted the latter and it landed her in prison. Others attempted the former and were charged with bigamy, or worse. Their lives were hard, and what memories would remain of

them years later? For Hall, orange eyes, a mugshot, and exile from a community. For many women who spent time in the Women's Ward, these might be as close to a legacy as they could hope for after they died.

"Menace to Society"

In the mugshot of Mary Mills, the 19-year-old girl with a dead father and a butterfly hairclip, she wears a

Immorality stood hand-in-hand with disease in a wartime hygienics poster, 1917.

SOURCE: FVZA.ORG

Right: Sad-eyed Mary Mills slumped for her prison mugshot, 1935.

SOURCE: ISHS

IDAHO STATE PEN
5231

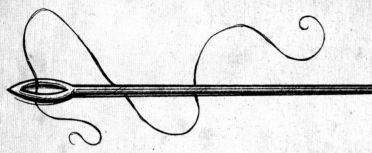

dress that bares her shoulders. When poor people might make dresses out of empty flour sacks, Mills's dress shines, even in the black-and-white photo, as though it is made of satin. During a conservative era of modest necklines, the front of her dress plunges. But the look in her eyes is not one of seduction, nor is it one of defiance or anger; it is a look of bewilderment, perhaps mixed with fear.

The pairing of butterfly clip and revealing dress confuses the viewer: woman or girl? It is even more troubling in the juxtaposition of evening outfit with hair that looks as though it has not been washed in days: oily, matted to her head, one wayward curl clinging to her left temple. The cut on her chin looks recent, and blotches that look like sores or bruises are scattered across her face.

In the three years following her father's sudden death, Mills is thought to have veered from one side of the state to the other. She spent time at an institution for children and youth 200 miles away from her home, near the eastern edge of Idaho in St. Anthony. Historical records variously refer to the place as a reform school, an orphanage, and even an "industrial school." Did her mother have her sent there rather than simply turning her daughter out onto the street? No records survive to offer hints as to when the girl arrived there or how long she stayed. As if by magic she next turns up 300 miles west, bouncing between the small town of Emmett and the nearby urban hub of Boise. By now her mother and brother may have left Gooding. The two of them left Idaho, moving far away to Los Angeles, without taking Mary with them.

Mills appears to have been thrust into the world with no way to get by. Perhaps at the school/reformatory/orphanage they taught her to clean, sew, and cook, but not much else. In Emmett, she turned to the most obvious and perhaps the only way to support herself.

Mills was never charged with prostitution. Before going to prison, she racked up a long list of crimes, including vagrancy. Still an adolescent, she was able to find shelter by living with a series of men. Prostitution is trading sex for money. "She had no apparent means

The sudden death of a father-provider was the beginning of the end for Mary Mills and other future inmates. Top left: Idle fingers took to sewing in lieu of vocational training. Left: Prom night sex leads to a back-alley abortion in *Street Corner*, released in 1948.

SOURCE: FILMPOSTERS.COM

of livelihood," says a probation document, "except by living with various men." That's not prostitution; today it is called survival sex — trading sex for shelter, for food, and perhaps for clothing. Safety and security until the man grows tired of that dress, that hair, and it becomes time to head back to the local nightclubs and find another man who is, in the words of a prosecuting attorney, "of a rather low moral character."

There are no records of any witnesses for the defense. However, almost as an afterthought, the same prosecuting attorney notes in Mills's record, "Doctors have reported to me that she is of very low intelligence and should probably be committed to a Feeble Minded Institute." But that never happened, and the acknowledgment seems to have begun and ended there; the girl was never institutionalized apart from being imprisoned. Even in light of her being deemed "feeble minded," she was judged a menace to society. This although officials also concluded that "she has no criminal tendency." She did, however, have "no moral standards whatever," not mitigated by her developmental issues. The ignored recommendation for sending Mills to an institution ended with "if her disease is ever cured." It seemed one of the men on whom she had turned to for support had given her a sexually transmitted disease.

More men showed up at the local health department with symptoms, claiming Mary Mills was the one who had given them venereal disease. (The specific disease was never identified in the available records.) At 19 years old Mills was arrested in Boise, just after Christmas 1935, on the charge of Exposing Another Person to the Infection of a Dangerous Disease. She spent almost a year in the Idaho State Penitentiary, turning 20 years old behind bars. None of the men associated with Mills were ever charged with any crime.

In Idaho, as in America, morality was narrowly defined, contributing to a system of class stratification that punished the poor more than the wealthy and women more harshly than men. From 1887 to 1968, of the 216 women confined at the Idaho State Penitentiary, 15 served time for chastity offenses that criminalized sex out of wedlock. Enforcement fell especially hard on the widowed, the diseased, victims of incest, broken families, and women without men to spring them from jail. It was a society of few distinctions between violent and victimless crimes. Women detached from men were denounced as "low class" and a "social menace," imprisoned rather than protected. Women in prison paid the price.

County jails rather than prisons held most women deemed subversive for breaking morality laws.
SOURCE: LIBRARY OF CONGRESS

Karen Benning, MFA, is a writer whose essays and poetry have appeared in *Michigan Quarterly Review, New Ohio Review, Boulevard, The Chattahoochee Review, The Morning News*, and other literary publications.

A porcelain washbowl and a small gray jar of disinfectant were among the evidence used to convict the nurse-cum-abortionist Lena Proud. Prosecutors alleged she was regionally known for running an "abortion mill" out of her house in Homedale. Left: Sketch from Proud's prison journal, about 1954.

Native Americans were never more than 2 percent of Idaho's state population but fully 12 percent of state prisoners in the Women's Ward. Nationwide, by 2000, Native American females under the age of 18 faced a higher risk of incarceration than young offenders from any other ethnic group. Pictured: Shoshone-Bannock girls pose in their kitchen aprons at the Fort Hall Presbyterian Mission School, about 1901.

SOURCE: ISHS

32 Cells: An Art Gallery

"History develops, art stands still," E.M. Forster wrote. While our historical take on prisons develops, art stands still in historical moments, telling stories in ways history books cannot. The 32 Cells Art Show, an annual exhibition, invites the Boise-based Swell Art Collective to glean historical meaning from 32 inmate biographical files. Ranging from the irreverent and whimsical to the pensive and innovative, each artwork is a visual comment on a prison now empty of convicts in a stark yet ever-changing historical-cultural site.

Think Good, Think Hollywood, by Noble Hardesty, 2018. (Ruth Ellen Sekinger)

Fecund, by Nancy Panganiban, 2018. (Josie Kensler)

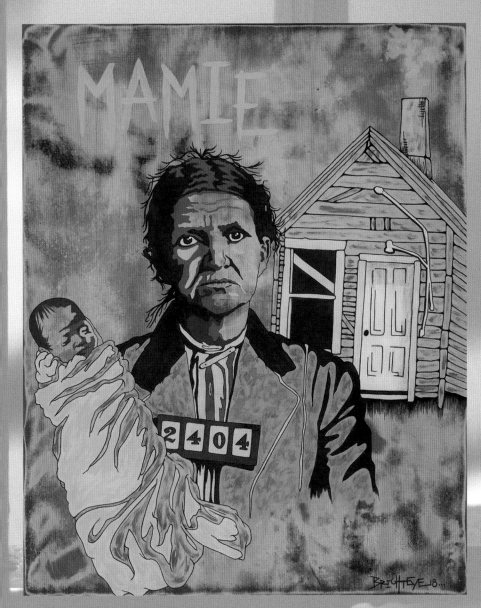

Mamie, by Chelsi "Brighteye" Benger, 2018. (Mamie Ross)

Calla Ghost, by James McKain, 2018. (Alwilda Reems)

Untitled, by Julia Green, 2017. (Marjorie Bess)

Untitled, by Julia Green, 2017. (Joy DeCheverieux)

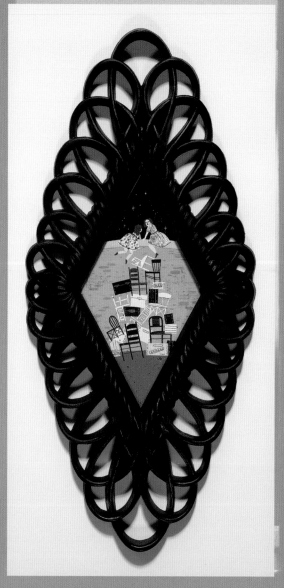

Untitled, by Julia Green, 2017. (Escape)

Breakfast with Verna, by Lance Brown, 2017. (Verna Keller)

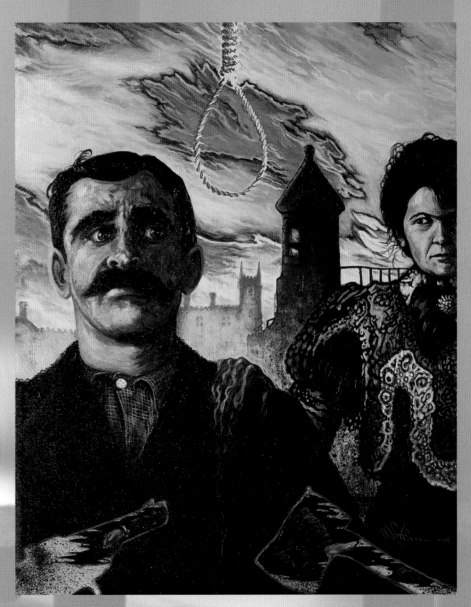

Done to Death, by Mike Flinn, 2018. (Jennie Daley and Fred Bond)

Memories, Hopes, by Nicolet Laursen, 2019. (Lula Ann Shreve)

Singing Thief of the Night, by John Irwin, 2019. (Mildred Knox)

Forgery in Leather, by Carri Sue Anderson, 2019. (Louise Alice Miller)

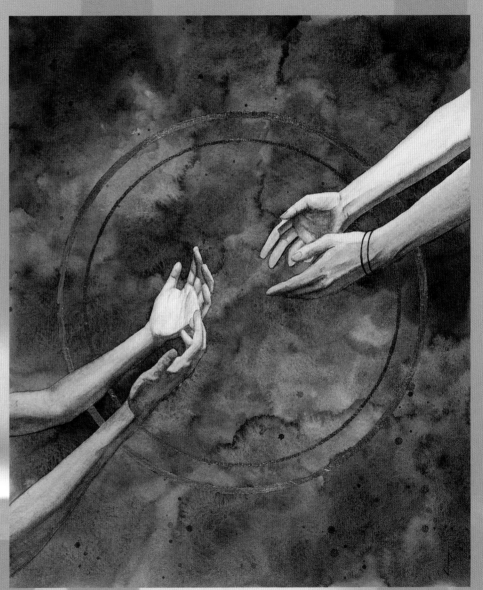

Samaritan, by Stuart Holland, 2018. (Lena Pink Proud)

The Idaho Children's Home in Boise, founded in 1908, cared for the children of at least 12 Women's Ward inmates. Mamie Ross of Cassia County, arrested for burglary, left her 2-week-old daughter at the home in 1916. Pictured: Children pose in the home's spacious parlor, 1934.

SOURCE: ISHS

4

Helpmates and Thieves

Women serving time for theft broke the rules, but even they hewed to conventional ideas of women in relation to men and to society.

By Anna Webb

The women who served time in the Idaho State Penitentiary Women's Ward were, like many female felons, beholden to societal strictures that made them second-class citizens when it came to their legal rights. These women had often served as helpmates to men up to no good. They were tough, yet remained vulnerable and confined to the will of men, often against their own best interests.

The criminal world paralleled law-abiding society in which women and men often perceived morality and justice in different ways. Carol Gilligan's *In a Different Voice*, a feminist classic published in 1982, argued that male reasoning is based on finite and less nuanced principles of justice — a bifurcated view in which criminal acts, morally and legally, are simply right or wrong. Female moral reasoning, said Gilligan, is more likely to be grounded in nurturing and caring for others. Stories from the Women's Ward reflect that division of thought.

Willing Partners in Crime

In poring through the stories of the women serving time for theft in Idaho, we see women committing criminal acts as part of a group or in partnership with men. Why did they do it? Some looked to impress, whereas others were trying to solidify relationships. Still others were confined by poverty and desperation long before their crimes sent them to the penitentiary.

Consider the story of Mary Allen, an illiterate mother of four. Her mugshot, showing her upswept hair and proper shirtwaist, resembles a studio keepsake, save for the inmate number, 1187, pinned to her chest. In 1905, she and her husband Arthur each received a four-year sentence for burglary. Their haul of stolen goods included several jars of fruit, hams, and a copper washtub. The Allens' part in a larger theft ring involving other accomplices explains the seemingly harsh sentence. Mary Allen served three years before earning parole.

Hattie Douglas and her partner Sam Ireland belonged to "the worst gang of horse and cattle thieves that we have had to deal with in recent years," according to the Jefferson County prosecuting attorney. In 1921 the Virginia-born Douglas went to prison for stealing a two-year-old black stallion in Mud Lake. No known prison mugshot exists, but records indicate that Douglas stood just over 5 feet tall, had bad teeth, and had a facial profile described as "Roman."

Despite her history as a thief, Douglas had just $1.75 in her pocket when her sentence of one to 14 years began. The state paroled her after a year-and-a-half on the condition that she return to Jefferson County where the sheriff, George Lufkin, could keep an eye on her. Once released, Douglas faced limited options. She quickly fell back in with Ireland and his gang.

In 1925, Lufkin and the Jefferson County prosecuting attorney penned a letter to Idaho governor C.C. Moore,

Left: Mary Allen's crime spree of 1905 included the theft of fruit jars and ham.
SOURCE: ISHS

Below: A black stallion from Mud Lake incriminated tiny Hattie Douglas and her tough gang of cattle rustlers.
SOURCE: LARAINE DAVIS FROM PEXELS

Cattle thief Sam Ireland hid out in a sheep wagon with Hattie Douglas. In 1925, while police searched for the couple, Douglas left Ireland stranded, speeding away in his car.

SOURCE: ISHS

Ellen Vance and Althalia Bybee shopped and tried on shoes while their husbands stole four suits from a store in Jerome. Pictured: Vance (left) and Bybee, partners in crime.

SOURCE: ISHS

asking that Douglas's parole be terminated. Douglas, said the authorities, had signed just one check-in report since her release. She was consistently "insolent and defiant," consorting with lawbreakers (Ireland), and conducting herself "in a manner that is highly obnoxious to all respectable citizens." The prosecuting attorney of Butte County, where Douglas and Ireland had been living in a sheep wagon, also weighed in. Douglas had been dressing in men's clothing, he said. Douglas and Ireland, he wrote, "have had the community in which they lived terrorized."

Plans were under way for Douglas's return to the penitentiary when Sam Ireland was arrested. This, at long last, may have ended Douglas's association with her partner and given her a kind of freedom. That very night, reported Sheriff Lufkin in a letter to the warden at the penitentiary, Douglas "took the said Sam's car and left for parts unknown." Rumors suggested she fled north to Canada. Others said they caught a glimpse of her in nearby Medicine Lodge. "We will notify you as soon as we find her," wrote the sheriff, "no matter how long we have to wait." Authorities never saw Douglas again.

Ellen Vance committed criminal acts not only with her husband but with another couple down on their luck in the midst of the Great Depression. Vance's black-and-white mugshot shows a woman with striking eyes — they were blue, according to her file. She wore her hair in classic finger waves. Vance and her husband lived in Idaho Falls. They made friends with the Bybees, another young couple. The Vances and the Bybees hatched a plan to make extra money by stealing men's suits and selling them. Their target: Tingwall's General Store in the farming town of Jerome. One May day in 1936, the four entered the store. The women distracted the clerk by asking him about shoes while the men made away with four suits. Later, when authorities apprehended the couples, they found 24 more stolen suits in their car. Courts convicted all four and sent them to the Idaho State Penitentiary.

Vance may have been a convict, but like other women of the era, her familial and maternal responsibilities continued. After serving close to a year of her sentence, she asked for parole, citing her ill mother and David, her 10-year-old son in need of care in Idaho Falls. Vance's prison file holds long letters from her mother written in dense, spidery handwriting, addressed to "my dear little girl." One, written in what was surely a dark, icy late January, read, "I have been thinking of you all day and wishing you were home. I sit in my chair lots of days all alone while David is in school."

Vance wrote the parole board: "I deeply regret having ever been implicated in this most unfortunate affair. I promise that my life will be ever that of a respected and law-abiding citizen." She did not mention her husband.

Son of a Problem

Boise City clerk Angela Hopper represents another trope of traditional womanhood — a mother determined to support and protect a son at all costs, even if that meant breaking the law. Hopper is a compelling figure for many reasons. Physically imposing, she stood 5 feet 9 inches tall and weighed 200 pounds. Photographs of Hopper reveal a strong face and intense gaze.

Beginning in 1923, just a few years after she became city clerk, money began disappearing from city coffers. This continued for a decade. According to records, Hopper embezzled more than $78,000, or $1.5 million-plus in 2020 dollars. Curiously, considering the amount she stole, Hopper lived modestly, even subsidizing her city salary by teaching music and English lessons. She did, however, dote on her son John. The *Idaho Statesman* described him in several stories as a "playboy" and ran a memorable photo of him in full dandy mode sporting a pencil-thin mustache, a wild shock of hair, and an open-collared shirt. Investigators found large unexplained deposits in his bank accounts.

Boise's Romanesque City Hall at 8th and Idaho, about 1925.
SOURCE: ISHS

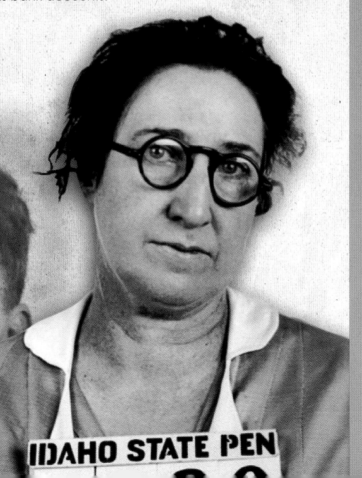

Angela and John Hopper, convicted mother and son, 1933.
SOURCE: ISHS

The 1863 O'Farrell cabin on Fort Street. Right: O'Farrell house at 420 W. Franklin, completed in 1892.

Angela Hopper's story is complicated by her privileged upbringing. Her parents, John and Mary O'Farrell, were Boise pioneers. O'Farrell Street in Boise's North End bears the family name. The O'Farrell cabin, considered the oldest residence in the city, still stands on Fort Street. The much grander O'Farrell mansion — Hopper's home during her childhood and until her arrest — stands nearby on Franklin Street.

Hopper lived a genteel life in turn-of-the-century Boise, a life very different from those of most women at the penitentiary. The *Idaho Statesman* is filled with mentions of Hopper — vying for the title of state fair queen, excelling in music and needle arts, and becoming valedictorian of her class at St. Teresa's Academy (the predecessor of Bishop Kelly High School). Ironically, considering what was to come, Hopper's valedictory focused on the school motto, "virtus et veritas," or virtue and truth. Newspaper mentions of Hopper continued into her adulthood, including her wedding to Edward Hopper at the family mansion in 1907, a spectacular lilac bush growing in her yard on Franklin Street, and the green rose she displayed on her desk at city hall to mark her Irish roots on St. Patrick's Day.

In 1933, Ada County courts convicted Angela Hopper of embezzlement. The *Idaho Statesman* called the case the "sensation of the year." John Hopper was convicted of receiving stolen property. Despite the convictions, Angela Hopper would never give her son up by revealing where the money went, even later when there were hints that such an admission might shorten her sentence.

By all accounts, John Hopper may not have warranted his mother's devotion. After his release on the stolen property charge, with his mother still in prison, he racked up a string of petty crimes. In 1937, he severely beat his aunt, his mother's sister Theresa O'Farrell, with whom he lived in the family home. She was found semi-conscious in the yard, along with copious amounts of blood and a broken platter in the kitchen.

Angela Hopper's fortunes continued to spiral downward. Authorities sent John Hopper to the State Hospital South in Blackfoot, formerly the Idaho Insane Asylum, on a charge of inebriety, or habitual drunkenness. The family home was sold. A *Statesman* story in 1937 described prison officials allowing Angela Hopper a brief release under guard to tend to her affairs. Warden William Gess made the concession "because everything in the house had been mortgaged and it seemed only reasonable that

Mrs. Hopper be allowed to look over her personal belongings." John Hopper received parole short of his two-year sentence and, according to the paper, decamped to California to sell cars in Los Angeles.

Angela Hopper continued to petition for parole. She cited her age, 54, and her desire to return to the workforce while she still could to repay her debts. In 1938, some five years into her one- to 10-year sentence, she wrote, "Since here, I have lost my beloved parental home and holdings, leaving me pauperized. . . . I certainly, by far, am not as black as painted." Hopper received a conditional parole after family friends in San Francisco offered her a place to live and a "good secretarial position."

One nod of kindness toward Hopper came from Mrs. E.J. Cummings, who penned the *Statesman* column "Through Eyes of the Farm Wife." "Idahoans can sincerely wish Mrs. Hopper a happy, peaceful Christmas," wrote Cummings shortly after Hopper's parole. "She has paid more than the average Idaho prisoner. If her sacrifices make a man of her son, she may yet become a proud and happy mother."

Angela Hopper outlived her troubled son by two years. One can only imagine how she took the news of his death.

Left: O'Farrell sisters, from left, Theresa, Angela, and Eveline, about 1899.
SOURCE: ISHS

Hopper embezzled more than $78,000, or $1.5 million-plus in 2020 dollars.

Idaho commissary coins, a currency for the male prison, about 1950.
SOURCE: ISHS

County sheriffs mostly tolerated games of dice and cards in roadside gambling houses. Idaho allowed Vegas-style slot machines (right) from 1947 to 1953.

Kootenai County deputy treasurer Minnie Farr embezzled nearly $9,000 to cover her gambling problem.

SOURCE: ISHS

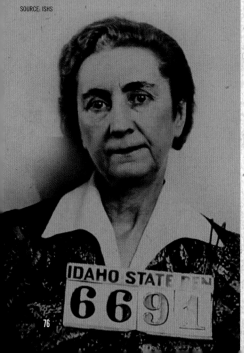

IDAHO STATE PEN
6691

The Rescued Hopeless

In keeping with a society that saw women as the weaker sex, the perception of criminal women as victims prevailed. Women, it could be reasoned, easily fell prey to bad circumstances. Some women inspired public sympathy in a way that's hard to imagine had their crimes been committed by men. In some cases, this public outcry helped shorten their sentences.

Minnie Jane Farr, an embezzler, looks every bit the mild-mannered public servant or elder aunt in her mugshot. Farr acted alone, a rarity among the women convicted of theft, but she stands out because of the sympathy she inspired. Farr served as the Kootenai County deputy treasurer in Coeur d'Alene in the 1940s. She had a gambling problem and, over the years, used her position to steal $9,000 to support her habit. Did society abandon her? Quite the opposite. More than 200 community members signed a petition asking for Farr's early release based on Kootenai County's past leniency for similar crimes. What's more, they raised $9,000 to repay the county so that Farr didn't have to. Another friend deposited $100 into Farr's prison account "not as a loan but as a gift." A Coeur d'Alene lawyer (unpaid) wrote in support of her parole, explaining that Farr had a "blameless record and a very creditable one" but that she was a mere "victim of the attraction of gambling machines." She served just eight months of her one- to 10-year sentence.

Horsethief Ida Belle Laherty, born in Washington in 1887, committed her crime at the behest of a man who abandoned her. Public sympathy for her swelled.

Laherty was one of the youngest inmates to serve time at the Idaho State Penitentiary. She grew up in a troubled home where her stepfather beat her. She left home at 15 and fell in love with a man named William Lewis. Lewis hatched a plan to have young Laherty hire a team of horses from a stable in Moscow and ride, alone, to Sprague, Washington, a distance of some 80 miles. He would meet her there and the two would sell the stolen horses. Laherty drove the team to Washington, but Lewis disappeared. Authorities arrested 16-year-old Laherty and charged her with grand larceny. Laherty, whose prison mugshot shows an impudent but undeniably beautiful face, went on trial in 1902 without the support of family or friends in the courtroom. The public took notice. The local branch of the Woman's Christian Temperance Union — the group that worked to enact "No Liquor Sundays" in Boise that same year and would, in 1910, install the bronze drinking fountain in front of Boise City Hall — sent petitions with more than 375 signatures to the Idaho State Board of Pardons pleading on Laherty's behalf. She received a one-year sentence.

The community continued to voice concerns about Laherty's age. The board received a new petition for her release with what the paper described as "an enormous number of signatures, including those of every member of the seventh legislature." After serving three months of her sentence, Laherty was released from prison.

Susie Duffy's community also stood by her. Duffy, a doe-eyed African American girl of 17, claimed to be a housekeeper in Lewiston on her prison intake form. In 1903, she received a three-year sentence for stealing $1,020 from a man named Frank Norris. The *Lewiston Teller* detailed the crime. According to the newspaper, Duffy had been working as a prostitute and had apparently "boasted of having touched Norris for $1,000." She fled to Oregon, but authorities extradited her back to Idaho where she stood trial.

Duffy petitioned for pardon in 1904. The application states that she was convicted on "very slim evidence" and "by parties to whose advantage it was to have her convicted in order to shield themselves." The document also noted that she suffered from epilepsy and lung issues and would likely perish in prison without proper medical care. Her inmate file includes a chart noting scars on her chest, her hip, her inner thighs, and her knee.

A model prisoner, Duffy developed "consumption," or tuberculosis, and was pardoned on the recommendation of the prison doctor. Boise's African American community, then representing less than 1 percent of the city's population, rallied and raised enough money to buy Duffy a ticket on the train to Kansas, where she had family. She left town the same day she was released.

Someone's Mother

Mamie Ross elicited as much sympathy as anyone. Her case also shed light on the struggles of convicted women with young children when her path crossed with Moses Alexander, the governor of Idaho.

Born in Albion, a tiny town in south-central Idaho in 1876, Ross, her second husband Daniel, and their blended family of eight children lived in squalid conditions. "Mrs. Ross has no home," proclaimed the *Idaho Daily Statesman* with the editorial tone so common in news stories of the time. The 10 members of the Ross family were living in "a rented lean-to," measuring about 8 by 14 feet. Most of the Rosses suffered from what the paper described as a "loathsome disease."

Boise's Woman's Christian Temperance Union petitioned against adult prison for juvenile offenders. Pictured: Boise's WCTU fountain and the union's trademark saloon-smashing ax.

SOURCE: BOISE CITY, NATIONAL MUSEUM OF AMERICAN HISTORY

Left: Susie Duffy entered prison with epilepsy and tuberculosis. Parole came with her promise to return to family in Kansas.

SOURCE: ISHS

77

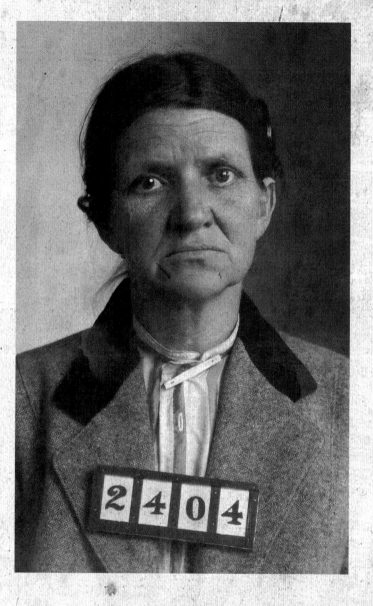

In 1916, authorities broke up a gang of thieves they believed had been operating around Albion for many years. They arrested Daniel Ross and sons, J.D., Leo, and Orville, for burglary. A search of the rented lean-to uncovered stolen items ranging from a pencil to sacks of wheat hidden between layers of the Ross children's bedding. Mamie Ross was charged with receiving stolen goods, though she claimed she had only stored the goods, quite unaware of their origins. On trial in Twin Falls, she pled guilty to the charge on the advice of her Albion lawyer, who told her such a plea would result in a lighter sentence. As a *Statesman* article noted, the trial judge urged her to get new counsel. He offered to appoint a lawyer for free. But Mamie Ross held to her original plan and received a sentence of six months to five years. The men in the Ross family were also sentenced to prison at the Idaho State Penitentiary.

Mamie Ross showed up to begin serving her sentence accompanied by Margaret Helen, her 2-month-old daughter. Margaret Helen, according to reports, had weighed just two pounds at birth. The prison was not equipped to house a baby. Mamie Ross was forced to leave the girl at the Children's Home, founded in 1908 to care for orphaned, abandoned, and neglected children. (Note: The institution changed in the 1960s when federal legislation began to favor a foster care system over orphanages, but the historic building still stands at 740 Warm Springs Ave., not far from the Old Idaho Penitentiary site.)

The newspaper of the day ran with a dramatic headline: "Mother Parts from Babe at Prison Gate." As the story read, "A pathetic scene was enacted at the Children's Home (Foundling) society Friday afternoon when a sobbing little woman parted with her two-months-old babe, leaving the infant in a dainty basinet (sic) in the nursery of the Children's Home, while the mother was taken to the penitentiary where the prison gates closed behind her."

The paper quoted Warden John Snook: "Had we had any kind of quarters for women at the penitentiary I should have permitted the mother to have her babe. but (sic) we have just one room and in this room are five women, two of them are diseased, and I did not think it well for the child to be left in this environment."

It happened that even before the Ross case, Snook had asked the Idaho State Legislature for money to expand the women's lodgings. The legislature had agreed to $1,500 for the expansion but Governor Moses Alexander (whose grand Queen Anne–style house stands at 304 W. State St.) vetoed the request believing it was unnecessary because of the small number of female inmates at the prison. The spectacle of Mamie Ross surrendering a baby to the Children's Home caused a public outcry. Criticism fell heavily on Alexander because of his veto. In response, the governor granted Ross a reprieve just five days after her original incarceration so that she could care for her baby as well as her other small children who had been left in the care of relatives. The paper noted that Ross collected Margaret Helen en route to the train station. A reporter asked Ross what she expected to

do once she was back home in Albion. "The first thing I hope to do is to get my children under my own roof again," said Ross. "Our things are still in the house that we rented. What I shall do after that I do not know."

Entrance gate to the Idaho State Penitentiary off Boise's Warm Springs Avenue, about 1912. Above: Prison guard's badge, about 1950.
SOURCE: ISHS

She continued to profess her innocence and that of her husband. They had never been in trouble before, she told the newspaper. Both paid the penalty for their sons' crimes. "It has been a terrible lesson to them," she said, "not only to suffer for what they did but to see us suffer also when they knew we were innocent." Ross eventually received a full pardon.

Door locks confined women to cells each night about 10:30.

Freed to Be Shackled

Property crimes committed by women who served time at the Idaho State Penitentiary Women's Ward paint indelible imagery — stolen horses, purloined suits, sheep wagons, consumption, and gambling dens. Idaho women convicted of theft ran the gamut from Mamie Ross and her squalid lean-to to Angela Hopper and her famous lilacs growing on a shady street in a tony Boise neighborhood, to women such as Ida Laherty and Susie Duffy, who were mere teenagers when they committed their crimes. In all of these convictions, though, we see commonalities. These are women who stepped outside of society's bounds but still operated within the strictest limits of what it once meant to be a woman in Idaho. Those serving time at the Women's Ward shared a desire for better circumstances — sometimes for themselves, but often for someone else.

Whether because of beauty, or youth, or just plain hard-luck stories, the community, it seemed, couldn't quite stomach the idea of some women living behind bars. Societal norms made it all too easy to see these women as someone's sister, mother, daughter, or wife. Pity and societal constraints both confined and freed them.

Anna Webb, MFA, is a writer and communications specialist at Boise State University. Webb was a reporter at the *Boise Weekly* and the *Idaho Statesman* and is the author of *150 Boise Icons,* a book that marked the city's sesquicentennial in 2013.

Quilting was deemed therapeutic. Stitching and sewing, said prison reformers, would counter the isolation of cold confinement without access to the baseball and vocational programs that occupied men. Pictured: Handsewn quilt, Idaho State Penitentiary Women's Ward, 1950s.

SOURCE: ISHS

Dust storms drove migrants west during America's Great Depression. From 1930 to 1940, the Women's Ward population doubled to a total of 34 inmates. Pictured: Dust-stricken migrants in Idaho's Oneida County, 1936.

SOURCE: LIBRARY OF CONGRESS

5

Hard Times, Small Crimes

Poverty and physical abuse seeded crime.

By Carissa Wolf

A youthful, 23-year-old face solemnly stares from Billy Garland's 1935 prison mugshot. Bruises stretch across the grainy, black-and-white photo, darkening patches of skin on her cheeks and across her neck. Her intake form paints a picture the photo couldn't capture. Bruises, burn marks, and scars riddle all quadrants of her body.

She called a pimp her boyfriend. Did he scar her body and leave her face black and blue, jailers asked? Garland remained silent.

Who would listen if she did reveal the force behind her scars and bruises? In 1935 Nez Perce County, refuge and shelter for abused women were hard to come by, and Garland's family lived nowhere near Lewiston, Idaho.

Domestic violence shelters were few in Idaho during the Great Depression, an era of unemployment, dust bowls, and breadlines. And when hard times hit the nation, rural states felt the brunt. From 1929 to 1932, Idaho was fifth in the nation in falling family income. Wheat prices dropped to $.25 per bushel, sugar beets to $4 per ton.

While a nation struggled to put food on the table, the federal government responded with work relief via the Works Progress Administration, which put laborers back in the workforce building roads, dams, and trails, and working on other civic projects. Part of the New Deal's $5 million investment in Idaho was its Women's Work Program, which created work for

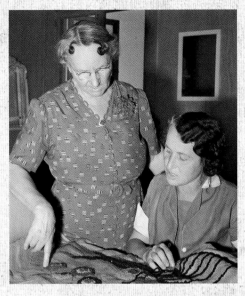

women sewing clothes, canning food, making bedding, nursing, and teaching.

The federal government's help came too late for Garland and many other female inmates serving time in the Women's Ward of the Idaho State Penitentiary for having forged checks to make ends meet. Their bruised, cracked faces tell the stories of migrants and survivors and of the times, places, and relationships that explain the reasons behind their crimes. Their roles remained narrowly defined, their opportunities few, and their dependence on patriarchal marriages as a form of survival almost guaranteed. Hard time greeted the ladies of the Women's Ward, and their stories remind us that too little came too late for too many.

Left: The Works Progress Administration provided job training for women as poverty seeded petty crime.
SOURCE: LIBRARY OF CONGRESS

Car theft, check forgery, and criminal association with a brutish felon sent Billy Garland to prison in 1935.
SOURCE: ISHS

85

Escaping Abuse

Social progress also came too late for Kay Elaine Montgomery. Montgomery, who preferred to go by Elaine, enjoyed a conventional upbringing by her adoptive parents in Gooding, Idaho, after a less than conventional 16-year-old mother gave birth to her at Boise's Booth Memorial Hospital in 1937. Montgomery's adoptive mother, Opal, remembered Montgomery as a happy child, but that began to change around the age of 15 when Opal said Montgomery started hanging out with the wrong crowd — "a bad group of friends," her mother reported. Around that time, her mother asked Montgomery to voluntarily commit herself to State Hospital South in Blackfoot for behavioral therapy. While undergoing therapy for unspecified reasons, Montgomery fell for the wrong guy.

Hughe Montgomery met Elaine at the state hospital sometime around 1953, shortly after serving time at the Idaho State Penitentiary for raping a minor. Montgomery's father pushed the couple to quickly marry. At the age of 16, Elaine said "I do" to the felon and convicted rapist, and they made their home in Twin Falls.

The two did not live happily ever after.

Montgomery soon gave birth to the first of three children and the abuse began. While caring for a toddler and infant daughter, the mental and physical abuse became so severe that Montgomery ran away to Boise after the birth of her youngest child in 1959. When that wasn't far enough, she ran even farther. Eventually Montgomery would zigzag across the continent with two friends and a book of bad checks in tow.

Montgomery ran, but she couldn't hide. Hughe zeroed in on Montgomery's location after months on the run and forced her to return to him. Broke, unemployed, and without a place of refuge, Montgomery complied and returned to Twin Falls.

When Montgomery returned, the abuse and violence resumed. When the beatings escalated, Montgomery fled again, this time to Pocatello. Along the way she forged and cashed six bad checks before prosecutors caught up to her. She skipped town before sentencing and kept moving and hiding around the country. In 1960 Hughe tracked down his wife once again and promptly turned her in to Pocatello police.

Montgomery told the court that she took full responsibility for forging and

English-American law once commonly held that a husband could beat his wife if the switch he used to beat her had no greater girth than his thumb.

Right: Beatings by her husband, a convicted rapist, forced Elaine Montgomery's flight from Boise. Check fraud sent her to prison at age 23.
SOURCE: ISHS

IDAHO STATE 10547 PENITENTIARY

of "lesbian activities." According to hospital doctors, Montgomery seemed to make progress at the facility that brought her and her abusive husband together less than 10 years earlier. But while hospitalized for a second time, Montgomery met another male patient, and the two escaped together in October 1961.

Montgomery's departures never lasted very long, and her escape from the hospital was no different. Authorities located her after only a few weeks. In April 1962 Montgomery was sentenced to the Idaho State Penitentiary's Women's Ward for parole violation where she served just over three years.

On the Margins

The most oppressed in early 20th-century Idaho — especially the poor, women and people of color, the mentally ill, and the abused — found themselves relegated to the margins of society and not in any position to buy safety, security, or justice. Class privilege afforded the accused the ability to post bail, a robust defense, and even a nice new dress to wear at court appearances. The same privileges afforded the abused the ability to disappear and the addicted a place to fall. But the ladies accused of some of the most down-on-their-luck crimes, who served hard time for petty crimes, couldn't even buy their own bread. And they certainly couldn't buy their way out of the Women's Ward at the Idaho State Penitentiary. How could Hattie Pearl Gardner, an addict,

cashing bad checks but said that she needed the money to escape from her abusive husband. After a nearly year-long prison sentence, parole evaluators questioned Montgomery's ability to succeed upon release because of her urges to wander the country and live independently. But beneath Montgomery's so-called free spirit and vagabond tendencies, a judge found a scared woman.

"She informed me that she just wants to be separated from her husband, who she fears, and the court found reason for that fear," the judge said, according to court transcripts.

Soon after the judge sentenced Montgomery to five years in the state penitentiary, she was transferred back to State Hospital South in Blackfoot for suspicion

Fifty-four arrests in nine different cities propelled Hattie Gardner's downward spiral. In 1956 in Nampa, the crime spree came to end with a forged check at a grocery store.
SOURCE: ISHS

Breadlines returned to the headlines in the late 1940s as too many workers for too few jobs plunged more than 40 percent of single-female households below America's poverty line.

a housewife, and a cook, convicted of cashing a forged $15 check at Nampa's Pick and Pack Grocery Store in 1956, ever purchase a single day of freedom?

Gardner's conviction set her apart from the "respectable" housewives of her day, but her life unfolded in long chapters defined by the hard luck and hard times that defined the stories of the typical female inmate in the Women's Ward.

Most of the women who walked through the Idaho State Penitentiary doors for fraud, forgery, or crimes related to passing bad checks were widowed, divorced, or single or had entered and exited multiple marriages. Most of the women with husbands and boyfriends had married young (most in their teens) and had accompanied their partners on crime sprees. Even more women had grown up without a father and lacked the safety net of post-adolescent parental support or a husband, almost guaranteeing a life of low-wage labor and admission into the ranks of poverty. Poverty became their crime. Need sentenced them to time.

Virginia Pugmire told prison psychological evaluators in 1955 that she could do any job, even the job of a man. The high school dropout worked on dairies, drove dump trucks, ran tractors, and irrigated fields. She scored high on intelligence tests administered by the prison. In her intake interview, Pugmire told officials that she also liked girls and aspired to become a physician because it was "time she started helping others instead of making a mess of her life and others." The bulk of Pugmire's evaluation then focused on her sexual orientation and the prospect

of releasing her to a reformatory in St. Anthony to address her attraction to other women. By the time prison officials interviewed her to determine her potential for parole, Pugmire had told them she would brush up on her shorthand so she could become a stenographer.

Somewhere along the way, ambition died inside many of these inmates.

Right: Prison officials fixated on Virginia Pugmire's masculine traits and sexual orientation.
SOURCE: ISHS

Sigmund Freud linked female crime to sexual abuse. Freudian theory, by mid-century, had become mainstream in criminology textbooks.
SOURCE: WIKIMEDIA COMMONS

The Idaho State Penitentiary opened its doors in 1872, and women entered in 1887, shortly after renowned gynecologist Dr. Edward Clark proposed at a conference that women were unfit for the rigors of higher education because the energy demanded by the brain of a college student would sap energy from the uterus and render a woman sterile. Or as physician Charles Megis said in 1847, "She has a head just big enough for love . . . she reigns in the heart . . . the household altar is her place of worship and service."

Some defied the adage that the altar of a woman remained in the home. Dorothy Ruth Cox had shown grit and determination early in life when she entered Northwestern University to study business

administration. She was expelled from school after she married Lyle W. Cox in 1929 and eventually replaced her academic record with a criminal record after her marriage turned to divorce and Cox turned to a nomadic lifestyle that eventually brought her to Idaho in the early 1960s. Cox spent her motherhood caring for a severely ill and disabled child. She told the courts and prison officials she felt "lost" after her

divorce and simply lived beyond her means. She used bad checks to bring some financial solvency into her life but began serving a 30-month sentence at the Women's Ward in 1963 for a series of bad checks that she wrote ranging from $20 to $400.

Bad Checks and Booze

In 1960, 15-year-old Gloria Jean Oliver married her step-cousin and the pair quickly had two children. Alcoholism and mental illness ran through Oliver's life, and the couple separated. Oliver lost custody of her children, who went to live at the Children's Home in Lewiston. While Oliver underwent treatment at State Hospital North in Orofino, the children were adopted. Prison records noted that Oliver didn't seem particularly distressed about the prospect of never seeing her children again.

The couple eventually reconciled after Oliver's discharge but were never able to eke out a living, always floating by with too little cash until they started forging checks ranging from $5 to $30 at grocery stores around Orofino. The grocery shopping eventually landed Oliver in the Women's Ward in 1964 where she served two years, four months.

Grocery stores remained popular destinations for the women convicted of check fraud and forgery. They often passed bad checks totaling less than $20.

For Barbara Burrell, a single, Holiday Motel worker in Caldwell, a forged $10 check that she cashed at a Boise grocery store netted her a 13-month stay at the

The forging of checks sent a total of 51 women to the Idaho State Penitentiary. Another 24 women served penitentiary time for the writing of checks with insufficient funds.

Left: A bad divorce and the strain of raising a disabled child haunted Dorothy Cox. A habitual offender, she bounced checks in four western states.
SOURCE: ISHS

Homosexuality implied deviance to prison officials in at least five female intake files.

Right: A deadly car crash in a canal plunged Phyllis Mink into poverty and alcoholism. Below: Joyce Brown Tanner, crippled by arthritis and malnutrition, forged checks to cover hospital bills.

penitentiary in 1964. Louise Alice Miller, a 52-year-old widow, told authorities that she never made enough money as a cook and so she forged checks to make ends meet. In 1965, she cashed a forged $20 check in Wallace and received a suspended sentence. But the forgery didn't stop, and Miller eventually served a six-year prison sentence from 1965 to 1972 for cashing a string of small but bad checks.

Virginia Pugmire cashed one of the more substantial singular bad checks worth $73.14 at the Bargain Barn in Pocatello and received a hefty sentence of five years thanks to an escape that tacked time on to her original sentence. Most of the women sentenced for forgery and check fraud typically served about a year-long sentence in the Women's Ward after which most quietly slipped into civilian life, new marriages, and law-abiding lives after their release.

Some cycled between prison and one of the state's psychiatric hospitals. One of these women was Pugmire, who spent a few weeks in 1955 at State Hospital South in Blackfoot for "perceived sexual deviation" after she told prison psychologists that she was sexually attracted to both men and women. After her discharge from the hospital, she violated her parole and quickly returned to the penitentiary, was released, and again violated parole on burglary charges. In 1958 Pugmire escaped during her final stay at the penitentiary before slipping into obscurity upon her release. The only public records she left behind were documents detailing a three-day marriage and a file at the Women's Ward, which exhaustively focused on her powerful, masculine

appearance and preference for what prison officials deemed "manly activities."

For others, incarceration followed tragedy. In 1964, Phyllis Mae Mink was traveling in a car with her common-law husband, two siblings, and two daughters when the automobile crashed into a canal. Her husband and daughters died. Mink spent the subsequent years surviving on alcohol until the alcohol landed her in prison on bad check and drunk and disorderly charges.

Joyce A. Brown Tanner never went without food, but what she ate left her empty. Tanner's alcoholic father abandoned the family during the Great Depression, leaving her single mother as the sole caretaker and breadwinner for seven children. The bread didn't stretch far in the Tanner household, and the family had no social safety net to wrap around their food insecurity.

IDAHO STATE
11258

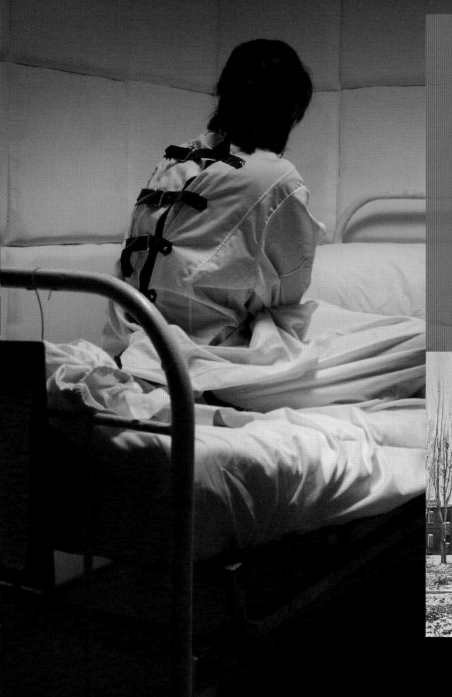

Pathologists probed the bodily roots of mental illness in every bump and lesion from a mad woman's womb to her brain. A "fire in the womb," called furor uterinus, was said to unleash hysteria and insatiable sexual urges. A malfunction at the base of the brain brought melancholy and hallucinations. As hospitals filled with chronic cases, some of them bedridden for life, the Idaho Territorial Legislature, in 1885, authorized an asylum for the insane in Blackfoot. Its first female convict was Margaret Hardy, transferred in 1895. Pictured: Straight-jacketed "hysteria"; State Hospital South, formerly the Blackfoot asylum, about 1894.

By 6 years old, Tanner had begun suffering from "nutritional arthritis" (most likely rickets), according to prison documents. By the time of her incarceration, her joints were so damaged they took on a bent shape.

Tanner, a fry cook, continued to suffer from ill health throughout her lifetime and in 1962, she was hospitalized. Then the medical bills began piling up. She realized she could not pay the bills and she

Nancy Christopher and two other female inmates escaped over the wall on a short ladder, a table, and boxes. Apprehended 12 days later, she went on to write editorials for *The Clock*. Far right: Roberta Schraeder of Portland, passing bad checks in Boise, boasted that Idahoans were easy marks.
SOURCE: ISHS

Three Women Flee Idaho Penitentiary

Boise —(UPI)— A hunt was on in Idaho today for three women who escaped from the state penitentiary Sunday night.

Warden L. E. Clapp said Virginia Lorene Pugmire, 22, Mary Ann Gardner, 21, and Nancy Frances Christopher, out of their cell the wall

needed money badly. She wrote $205 worth of bad checks and in a short time, traded her hospital bed for a prison bunk.

Nancy Frances Christopher's 1958 crime spree began in Las Vegas after several days of drinking with three

buddies and ended in Emmett, Idaho, after police apprehended her for cashing a $25 forged check at J.C. Penney.

The court sentenced Christopher to a six-year term, and she, like many of the mothers that dominated the population of inmates, would have likely been released early to tend to her two young children. Instead, Christopher jumped the prison wall and became notorious as one of the penitentiary's failed female escapees.

Roberta Blanche Schraeder's second husband, Ernest, spent all of their money on alcohol. The financial abuse forced Roberta, who suffered from chronic ill health that required two heart surgeries, to find another means of economic survival. Beginning in 1959, Schraeder was arrested three times in Portland, Oregon, for obtaining money under false pretenses. In 1964, she took her crime spree to Boise, where she cashed bad checks totaling $1,500. She later told officials that she didn't feel bad about her crimes, only that she was caught so soon.

Shirley Ann Harvey shared a similar story. She married young, as many of the few married women in the Women's Ward did. She was 16 years old when she married Claude Trout, a man who refused to do much of anything after he said his vows. He didn't work, and Harvey's waitress job barely allowed them to survive. In 1963, Trout began to encourage Harvey to pass bad checks so the two could eat while her parents paid their rent. Harvey passed bad checks for $5, $47, and $10 before receiving a three-year sentence at the Idaho State Penitentiary.

During times when a woman's economic independence was rare, women found themselves at the financial mercy of their husbands or fathers. And husbands like Frank J. Kennedy showed their wives and families little mercy. Freda Mae Starr married Frank at age 17, and the two spent the early 1950s having a total of five children. Starr occasionally worked as a maid, and the couple raised their family in cramped, unsanitary shared rooms, rarely sent the kids to school, couldn't afford to buy clothes, and once stole a car from a Welfare Department worker. The parents were often accused of child neglect and by 1965, Starr was serving time in the Women's Ward and Kennedy eventually called a federal prison home. All the children were placed in foster care during Starr's incarceration. It's not known if she ever saw any of her children between her release in 1966 and death in 1979.

Sisters in Crime

The 20th century widened the gap between the rich and poor in the United States. The haves became have-nots in the distances between the county jails and the cold prisons where the poor and unfortunate served their time. By the late 1950s, in the boozy check-bouncing era of Montgomery, Gardner, and Pugmire, 15 women crowded into the small women's cellblock in Boise. Rumblings of change rolled through as the women's liberation movement grew stronger. Today, in the country that far and away leads the world's prison population, Idaho nearly leads the nation with an estimated 209 of every 100,000 women in the criminal custody or supervision of state or federal courts. The state's prison population, annually, is now four times the entire 62-year population of the penitentiary's Women's Ward.

Shirley Harvey (top) was confined to her cell for a month for kiting letters over the wall to a boyfriend. She shared the ward with Freda Starr, accused of "immoral activities with men."
SOURCE: ISHS

Women's Incarceration
NUMBERS IN CUSTODY PER 100,000 WOMEN

Today incarceration extends beyond prisons and jails to many other systems of confinement. In *States of Incarceration: The Global Context* (2018), the Prison Policy Initiative lists Idaho as tied with Tennessee for the nation's fourth highest rate of female incarceration. In Idaho, for every 100,000 women, 209 are under court-ordered custody or supervision.
SOURCE: PRISON POLICY INITIATIVE

IDAHO	209
USA	133
EUROPE	90
CANADA	13

Homosexuals, perverts, and the insane could be sterilized under a 1918 Idaho law.

Rise in Women's Incarceration

Today, nationwide, there are more women in prison and jail than at any time in American history. Since 1980, the rate at which Americans imprison women has grown nearly 800 percent, more than twice the growth rate for males.

SOURCE: BUREAU OF JUSTICE STATISTICS: HISTORICAL CORRECTIONS STATISTICS IN THE UNITED STATES, 1850-1964; PRISON AND JAIL INMATES AT MIDYEAR SERIES (1997-2017), PRISONERS SERIES (1986-2018). WASHINGTON, DC

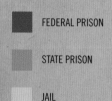

FEDERAL PRISON

STATE PRISON

JAIL

The Women's Ward had closed, its inmates relocated, by the time Congress and the U.S. Supreme Court recognized gender, analogous to race, as worthy of the 14th Amendment's equal protection under the law. Not until 1973 did the American Psychiatric Association remove homosexuality from its official *Diagnostic and Statistical Manual of Mental Disorders*. Not until 1994 did Congress empower law enforcement to prosecute spousal rape and domestic violence as sexual assault.

Garland, Montgomery, Gardner, and Pugmire didn't live long enough to feel the freedom of that progress. Nor did Joyce Tanner, crippled by arthritis, who fell through the economy's cracks long before a right to employment was written into the 1990 Americans with Disabilities Act. Disabled women like Tanner had few options besides passing bad checks. Trapped and isolated, they struggled against what sociologists have called a "matrix of domination." A phalanx of barriers to social advancement, its walls multilayered with norms and biases against the poor and disabled, the matrix fell especially hard on women detached. When a desperate woman did attach herself to a man, she often found herself linked to a deadbeat. Sometimes that man was a brute who lured a vulnerable woman into a romance with lawlessness resembling that of the gangsters Bonnie and Clyde.

"Oftentimes the lives of many of these women are intertwined with men who are persistent thieves or in other ways are 'losers,'" wrote sociologist and criminal historian Ruth T. Zaplin in *Female Offenders: Critical Perspectives and Effective Interventions*. "The world of these men tends to be an extremely patriarchal one in which women are regulated to subordinate roles [and] exploited or treated with indifference by their male partners," Zaplin noted.

Violence often marked the patriarchal relationship. It was a relationship Kay Elaine Montgomery couldn't run from and one that left bruises Billy Garland couldn't hide.

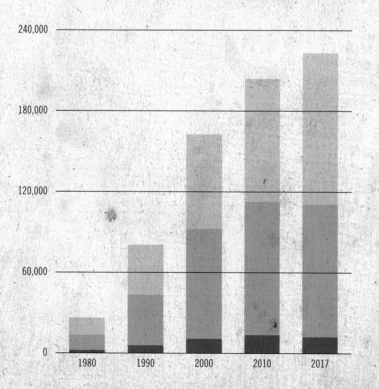

240,000				
180,000				
120,000				
60,000				
0				
1980	1990	2000	2010	2017

Carissa Wolf, MA, is a journalist, educator, and media activist, whose work has appeared in the *Washington Post*, the *Idaho Statesman*, and on National Public Radio. Wolf teaches sociology and communication at Boise State University.

Flying Devils (1933) ignited a media scandal after Warden George Rudd took his family to see the movie at Boise's Fox Theater (now the Egyptian on Main at Capitol). The outing included the Women's Ward's matron and its most notorious inmate, the husband-slayer Lyda Southard. "Humane treatment," said the warden, was his only motive. The warden had also allowed inmates, under supervision, to play tennis, attend dances, and visit ailing family members. Despite 156 inmates signing a petition calling for him to remain, the Prison Commission forced Rudd's resignation.

SOURCE: ISHS, RKO RADIO PICTURES

95

"*Our roses are blooming. Against a background of soft green lawn and weathered stone, they create a picture of bountiful splendor. The fragrance emitting from the different varieties mingle and rise to give forth to our home a breath of spring.*" *From The Clock, a prison newspaper, July 1959.*

SOURCE: ISHS

6

Prison Voices

Gender was ever-present in letters from prison and the social expectations through which prisoners measured their lives.

Compiled by the Old Idaho Penitentiary staff

A plea for freedom. A governor's pardon. A mother's salt tears of remorse. Documents mined from the archives show a slow unraveling of moralistic ideas about women and delinquent behavior. Others drip red with violence. Still others, mournful and raw, are windows through bars into hearts.

A Fiendish Grin

PRISON OFFICIALS STRUGGLE WITH CHILD-KILLER MARGARET HARDY, AS REPORTED IN THE IDAHO STATESMAN, MARCH 22, 1895.

Mrs. Hardy, the murderess who is serving life imprisonment in the Idaho penitentiary for killing her adopted daughter, a little negro girl, has given the prison officials no end of trouble. She started in with a glass swallowing exhibition.

For some time she has raved almost incessantly, her wild cries driving the officials and the convicts as well to distraction. [Guards] put her in the "bug house" where troublesome prisoners are kept. Her blood curdling cries were muzzled in the "bug house."

[Once] she gathered up her bed clothes and set them on fire. Mother Hardy's cell was like a furnace, and in one corner of it, crouching on the floor and peering through the flame and smoke, a fiendish grin on her deep-wrinkled face.

Shot Through the Heart

JENNIE DALEY, CONVICTED OF KILLING HER HUSBAND, TESTIFIES THAT THE DEED WAS DONE BY HER LOVER FRED BOND; FROM THE 1905 TRIAL TRANSCRIPT.

[Husband Charles Daley] asked me if I loved Freddie. I told him I did. [Charles] says, "Freddie, you hear that? . . . I guess my wife has no more use for me. The best thing I can do is to go."

[Charles] had taken his shoes off and was starting to put them on [when] Fred shot him. [Fred Bond, the lover] had shot all the shells out of the revolver. [Bond] took the hatchet out of the table drawer. He slapped him in the face with it. I guess it was in the face. I don't know where it was. He then just put the hatchet back in the drawer.

My husband was groaning very much. [Bond] then took another shell and put it in the revolver. Freddie then shot my husband through the heart. He died shortly afterwards.

I wrote a letter. Freddie asked me to. I sat up the rest of the night.

Downtrodden Humanity

GOVERNOR MOSES ALEXANDER PARDONS MAMIE ROSS, BELIEVING POVERTY WAS TO BLAME FOR HER CRIME, APRIL 1916.

Justice may have been dealt and the law vindicated but from the viewpoint of humanity and my idea thereof, this mother of an infant less than a month old has no business

Court documents dispute whether the pistol emptied into Charles Daley was fired by the victim's young wife or Fred Bond, her lover. Left: Jennie Daley, age 21, convicted of manslaughter. Below: A letter of pardon from an inmate file.

SOURCE: ISHS

PARDON

STATE BOARD OF PARDONS OF IDAHO

in the penitentiary. [This is not a precedent, but to help] the cause of down-trodden humanity [and] a soul who has been oppressed by environment and unfavorable opportunities in this battle of life.

Wishing You Crabs

CORA DUNN, WRITING FROM PRISON, DENOUNCES HER INFECTIOUS ACCOMPLICE, 1917.

You weren't satisfied getting me in jail and the penitentiary, but you have caused me to get crabs. For a solid month I have been itching and I said to the girl in here with me, "This is the most peculiar soil out here, it just sticks tight." She took a piece of that soil and cracked it and it was a crab. They have had such a [indecipherable] visit that they are fat and juicy, and they surely do crack. I wish I could send you some. It makes me so angry. I surely would like to give them to you.

Absolutely Innocent

LYDA "LADY BLUEBEARD" SOUTHARD SHOWS NO REMORSE; FROM THE SALT LAKE TELEGRAM, JUNE 22, 1921.

I am not worried. My conscience is clear and I have documentary proof of the causes of the death charged to me. I know I can clear myself. Life insurance was no object to me. I have had enough money. I am sorry there has been all of this publicity about the various charges. I would have returned voluntarily had I known I was wanted. I am particularly sorry that father and mother have been caused all this grief. I am absolutely innocent of all the charges and feel that the evidence will clearly establish this fact. I am ready for trial right now.

The clicking of Yale padlocks was a nightly reminder that guards had secured the cells. Right: Cora Dunn of Twin Falls hoped to return a parting gift from her lover.
SOURCE: ISHS

Right: A guard's shack and kitchen, about 1900, predated the women's cellblock. In 1912, the shack was razed for a two-story guardhouse.
SOURCE: ISHS

Sentimentality Breeds Chaos

WARDEN JOHN SNOOK, IN HIS 1925 REPORT TO IDAHO'S BOARD OF CORRECTIONS, QUOTES A TOUGH-MINDED PRISON CHAPLAIN.

Prison reform on the basis of sentimentality will never prevail. Sentimentalism is allied with emotionalism, which is unstable and as safe as shifting sands for the foundation work. Emotionalism in any institution will upset the whole institution and make for chaos, favoritism, and ridicule. A firm hand on the rudder, clearness of vision in the pilot, refusal to be swayed by selfishness, cunning, or personal aims of inmates or outsiders are required for successful prison management and to save reform from ridicule. The prisoner asks for justice and not for emotion, for a fair deal and not for favoritism.

Homosexual Tendencies

CONVICTED OF BIGAMY, DIAGNOSED AS A "HERMAPHRODITE [WITH] BOTH MALE AND FEMALE CHARACTERISTICS," DAISY PARSLEY PROMISES TO BECOME A PROPER CHRISTIAN LADY IN EXCHANGE FOR PAROLE, 1943.

Since I've come back [to prison for a second offense], there has been a complete change in my life. I'm letting my hair grow. I wear nice little dresses and wouldn't think of putting on a pair of slacks or being tomboyish. I'm a regular little lady.

I've been sewing ever since I've been back. I've made a set of five small sofa pillows, a dresser scarf edged with lace, four potholders and a bedspread that contains 54 square pieces that I cut and drew

and embroidered.

Last but not least, the thing that makes me happiest, is that I've given my heart to God and become a Christian.

If you give me one more chance. I'll go home to mother and lead a good Christian life. Also [I will] obey all the parole rules until after the war when my husband comes home. Then him and I will settle down together. I thank you in advance from the bottom of my heart with tears in my eyes and a prayer in my heart. I close by saying, please grant me my freedom.

Car theft, forgery, and overlapping marriages sent Daisy Parsley to reform schools and prisons in three western states.
SOURCE: ISHS

"An interesting feature of the prison is the kennel of bloodhounds used for tracking escaped prisoners. Standing on their hind legs they look over the high fences that surround them, and at the sight of a prisoner in striped clothes, they split the air with a chorus of howls that are little less than bloodcurdling. The dogs are Cuban and Russian breeds and said to be rare specimens of their race." From the Idaho *Statesman*, June 16, 1902.

SOURCE: ISHS

Hanging Naked

AN INTERVIEW WITH TURNKEY FRANK RICHARDSON, RECALLING THE 1950s AND THE PRANKING OF ANOTHER GUARD.

Old Cy Bradley lock the women up at 10:30 at night. I forget what the woman's name was. Cy was about a 65-year-old guy, never been married before in his life, you know, lived over here all of his life, and had no contact with the outside world at all except here at the pen.

[The inmate] just tormented that guy. He'd go over there and lock up at 10:30 at night, you know, she would get completely undressed and she'd be hanging on the bars, you know, with her feet and her hands like a monkey. They just loved to embarrass the guards.

Of course every time anything was said or anything was done you had to come back and write up a report. It would become a nightly occurrence with [the inmate] and old Cy Bradley.

Now, when Cy would be off on Saturday and Sunday, you know, when the other guard would go in there, they didn't mess with him. But Cy, they just loved to see him run out in a tizzy. The warden, you know, the only thing he could do was to tell the woman guard the next morning, "Hey, have a talk with them, tell them to leave Cy alone." She was a lifer, you know. All they could do was say, "Hey, please don't do that to Cy anymore."

Cold as Steel

NANCY "CHRIS" CHRISTOPHER SHARES HER REMORSE; FROM HER COLUMN IN THE PRISON NEWSPAPER THE CLOCK, SEPTEMBER 1960.

A woman inside prison walls is looked upon as cold as steel, but is she? Trying to analyze the heart of a woman in prison is like trying to see through a steel door. [She lives for] the hope of a new life and the hope that she can forget those cherished things that was once all she wanted in life. And if the people that helped cause this hurt could see her now, see the misery written in her face and know the pain in her heart, they could believe her when she says, "Never again will I trade my life of a loved and cared for wife to a woman of the wild side of life."

You don't have to be told the sister is ashamed to be seen with you. The husband cannot find it in his heart to give you that chance and the agency sees you only as a woman that has lost her right to be a mother.

Then the heart begins to steel itself and then the heartaches come.

Nerves Jangle, Tempers Flare

NANCY "CHRIS" CHRISTOPHER BEMOANS INCOMPATIBLE HOUSEMATES; FROM THE CLOCK NEWSPAPER, APRIL 1961.

Nerves jangle that never jangled before, tempers flare where hitherto there were no tempers. Day by day this goes on, and when release day arrives the relief from

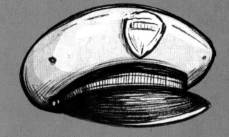

Guard hats were rarely tipped to unruly women. Left: Guard Josef Munch, German born, was a no-nonsense yard captain in the late 1960s.
SOURCE: ISHS

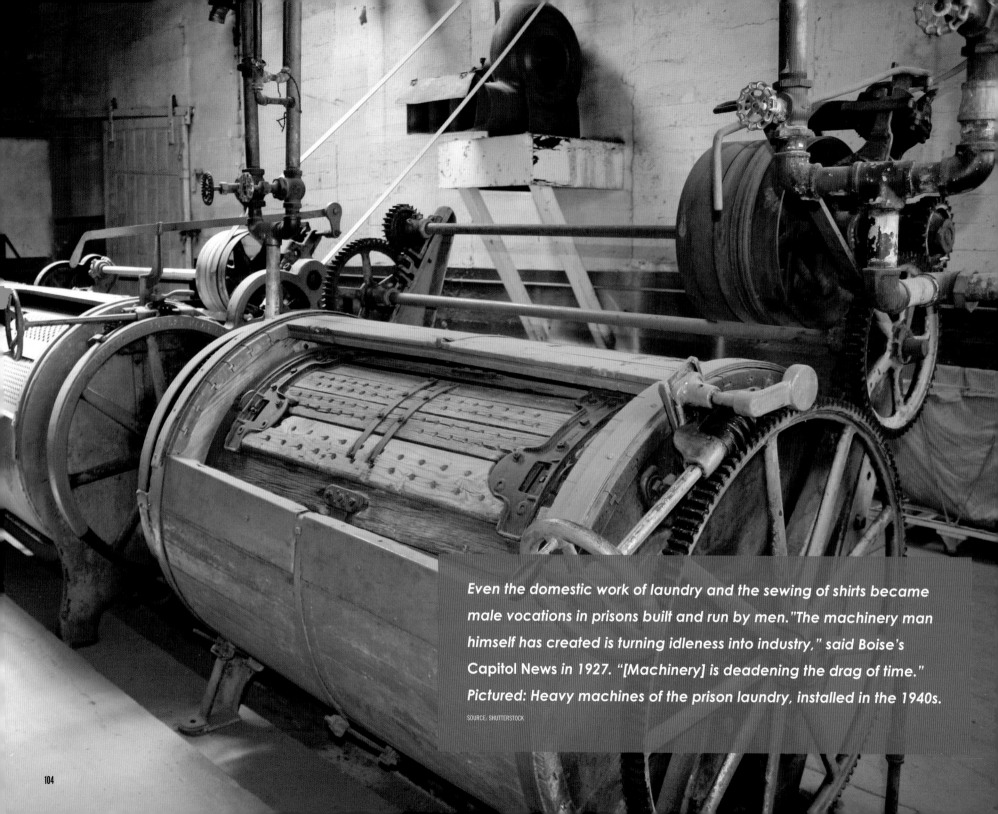

Even the domestic work of laundry and the sewing of shirts became male vocations in prisons built and run by men. "The machinery man himself has created is turning idleness into industry," said Boise's Capitol News in 1927. "[Machinery] is deadening the drag of time."

Pictured: Heavy machines of the prison laundry, installed in the 1940s.

SOURCE: SHUTTERSTOCK

pressure is so great the aftereffects could prove to be downright serious.

But what else can you do? You have to live with your other women inside. Ergo, you have to swallow pride, self-reliance, and sometimes common sense. It's a shame that many who have nothing in common must be placed together. How much better it would be if these incoming women could be screened and placed in their own category. It would relieve a lot of pressure and create a more congenial atmosphere.

One thing is certain; if incarceration doesn't teach you a lesson, the everlasting moans of "Bum Beef," "Poor Me," and "Injustice" will.

Trouble Ahead

THE STATESMAN *REPORTS WARDEN LOUIS CLAPP'S TESTIMONY ON PRISON OVERCROWDING, OCTOBER 18, 1964.*

Idaho's state penitentiary is nearly 100 years old. It shows its age. The warden says, "Conditions at the penitentiary are fast reaching a breaking point. Trouble of one kind or another can be expected when the population reaches or exceeds 500. The institution isn't physically capable of handling that many."

Clapp admits, as he looks back on riots that have occurred within the walls, that Idaho and the institution "have been lucky" that there were not others and of a more serious nature. The facilities for both men and women are strictly bad.

You Got a Number

EMILY McLAWS RECALLS HER WELCOME AT THE PENITENTIARY, 1965.

The sheriff brought us up in a car. I was the only woman, and then there was a couple of men prisoners. They brought us in. They took the men [to their] side, and they took us in [another] room and they went through our stuff, and after they went through our stuff, the matron Mrs. [Lulu] Rowan took me in another room and she was talking, she said, "All right, Emily, your number" (laughs) and she gave me a number. I looked at her and said, "What?" She says, "You ain't got a name anymore. You got a number. Now remember this." She said it back to me and I repeated it and she said, "Yes honey, you remember that. Anytime you come and go and that you give the number."

Remorse shared pages with gossip in editorials typed for *The Clock*. Left: Warden Louis Clapp. Below: Sandstone and steel frame the amber foothills.

Lulu Rowan, an experienced nurse, watched over the ward as matron, 1961-1967. Right: A volleyball retrieved from a roof prompted some raucous behavior.

SOURCE: *IDAHO STATESMAN*

Ladies Don't Wave

EMILY McLAWS RECALLS A WARDEN'S FRUSTRATION AFTER A RAUCOUS VOLLEYBALL GAME, ABOUT 1966.

We had a volleyball net out in back, and we'd go out and play volleyball and hit the ball over the wall and then they could call over the men to pick up the ball and throw it over and most of them would come to the gate and bring them in. And, we'd hit them up on top of the building and have the men come over and crawl up there and get 'em, throw them down to us. Finally [the guard] said the women would have to crawl up there and get them by ourselves.

So, [an inmate] crawled up one day to get them and she called down. She says, "You should see the good-looking man over there in the red shirt. He is really good looking." [She waved, yelling], "Yoohoo yoohoo." And she says, "Oh, he's waving back."

Of course then she got down off and [Mrs. Rowan, the matron] got a call. "All right, you girls," [said Rowan]. "All of you come in and sit down. The warden is coming over to talk to you." And so we all went in and we sat down and here come the guy in the red shirt, and it was Warden [Louis] Clapp.

"All right, girls," he said, "I know you don't like being here. Well, we don't like having you here anymore than you like being here, but you have to be here and we've gotta have you here. I wished you would just learn to behave like ladies. Ladies don't get up on top of the building and wave, you know."

So that put a stop to us going on top of the building. We just took the volleyball net down.

Filling an Aching Void

RUBY WALKER, DAUGHTER OF A 1925 INMATE, RESPONDS TO CONCERNS FROM THE OLD IDAHO PENITENTIARY ABOUT POTENTIALLY HURTFUL NEW INFORMATION IN HER MOTHER'S FILE, 1986.

Thank you for your compassion. It was sweet of you to express concern about perhaps having sent something hurtful. Don't worry though. I have lived my entire life with most of this knowledge, and nothing about it is painful to me. You see, I loved my mother and still do. She was a beautiful, warm, witty person who tried to worm her way into the arms and heart of someone, anyone, everyone, singly and altogether, who might be able to fill her acute need for love. I can remember some of her search, some of her attempts to fill what must have been an aching void, and I now wonder if many so called prostitutes are so very different from her.

Souping up hot rods and the chewing of gum in class were said to be sparks of Armageddon in the postwar pop psychology of juvenile crime. Pictured: A tawdry tale featured a women's prison in *One Girl's Confession*, 1953; *Hot Rod Girl*, a noirish film about delinquent teens, 1958.

SOURCE: MOVIEPOSTERS.COM

107

Idaho's brooding architecture of incarceration featured broad arches, round towers, castle battlements, and towering spires. Historians call the style Romanesque Revival. Pictured: Sandstone buttresses rib a turreted wall.

SOURCE: MARJORIE McBRIDE

7

IDAHO STATE PEN
4694

Lives in Confinement

A century of mugshots belies simplistic thinking about any one source of delinquent behavior or any one criminal type.

By Old Idaho Penitentiary staff

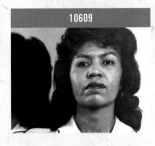

10609

AGUILAR, EDITH J.
Age 27, Grand Larceny
Nez Perce County, 1960
Served 8 mos.

Convicted for stealing a sewing machine from a Nez Perce Montgomery Ward. Formerly a nurse, Aguilar confessed she was too intoxicated to remember her crime.

9008

AINSWORTH, DORIS MAE
Age 24, Forgery
Twin Falls County, 1954
Served 10 mos., 27 days

Sentenced for forgery after writing a bad check and signing a fake name. Ainsworth was arrested on the run with her husband, an escaped convict.

1187

ALLEN, MARY
Age 32, Burglary, First Degree
Ada County, 1905
Served 3 yrs., 2 mos.

Convicted with her husband for robbing a neighbor. Law enforcement caught the couple with canned fruit and several hams taken from their neighbor's cellar.

11340

ANDERSON, AMBER MAE
Age 33, Burglary, First Degree
Kootenai County, 1963
Served 2 yrs., 9 mos., 15 days

Arrested on the side of the road during a police stop for intoxicated driving. In a search of Anderson's car, police found a book of stolen checks.

5788

ANDREWS, HELEN GRACE
Age 24, Forgery
Latah County, 1938
Served 8 mos., 21 days

Convicted of forgery after writing bad checks. The prison warden characterized Andrews as a weak woman under the bad influence of her dangerous husband.

12070

ANDREWS, JUDITH MARIE
Age 21, Issuing a Check Without Funds
Nez Perce County, 1966
Served 10 mos., 16 days

Sentenced for check fraud after violating probation. Andrews, while incarcerated, worked hard to find a job and earn an early release.

11512

ANNIS, JUDY LOUISE
Age 19, Robbery
Nez Perce County, 1964
Served 1 yr., 8 mos., 1 day

Convicted for stealing a purse from an elderly lady. Annis, who was abused and deeply troubled, attempted suicide multiple times.

12108

ANSTINE, DORIS LUCILLE
Age 41, Manslaughter, Voluntary
Kootenai County, 1966
Served 1 yr., 8 mos.

Charged with shooting her third husband. Anstine claimed she had suffered a beating and that the shooting was accidental.

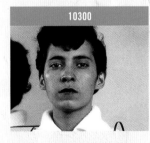

10300

ARCHULETA, ELEANOR VIVIAN
Age 21, Forgery
Bannock County, 1959
Served 1 yr.

Convicted for violating her probation. Archuleta had spent time in a state hospital for drinking, smoking, and delinquent behavior.

2529

ATKINSON, CORA
Age 30, Grand Larceny
Twin Falls County, 1917
Served 4 mos., 4 days

Convicted of thievery and delinquency. Bohemian immigrant, with gold teeth and multiple scars, Atkinson received the governor's pardon to care for her son.

Idaho Female Inmates by Number and Type of Crime, 1887-1968.

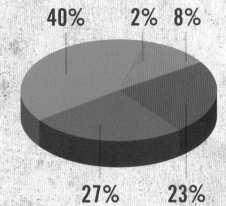

40% **2%** **8%**

27% **23%**

■ **VIOLENT CRIMES:** murder, manslaughter, deadly assault

■ **MORAL CRIMES:** adultery, bigamy, rape, induction to prostitution, venereal disease exposure, Mann Act, Prohibition laws

■ **THEFT CRIMES:** burglary, robbery, larceny, stolen property, embezzlement

■ **PETTY CRIMES:** insufficient funds, forgery, obtaining money under false pretenses

■ **OTHER CRIMES:** escape, arson, and damaging a jail

SOURCE: ISHS

In 1947, Boise police arrested Margaret Barney with her husband accomplice for breaking into homes, stealing wrapped presents from under Christmas trees.

2358

AYCOX, MAGGIE
Age 36, Manslaughter, Voluntary
Bannock County, 1915
Served 1 yr., 5 mos., 19 days

Convicted of shooting a former boyfriend at his home in Pocatello. Prosecutors characterized the shooting as an act of revenge by a woman scorned.

9431

BARKER, MARY ALLENE
Age 36, Unlawful Check Writing
Payette County, 1956
Served 1 yr., 5 mos., 20 days

Convicted of writing a bad check to a Payette grocery store. Arrested with a male companion, Barker confessed to the fraud as an act of desperation.

8747

BARNES, MARY ALICE CANNON
Age 25, Manslaughter, Voluntary
Bannock County, 1953
Served 2 yrs.

Convicted of shooting an intruder, having violated probation by carrying a concealed handgun. Court documents indicated the shooting was in self-defense.

7323

BARNEY, MARGARET M.
Age 21, Robbery
Ada County, 1948
Served 3 yrs., 5 mos., 3 days

Sentenced for breaking into homes and stealing Christmas gifts. Barney and fellow inmate Verna Keller escaped the Women's Ward to "prove it could be done."

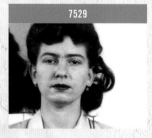

7529

BARRETT, FLORENCE MONIENE
Age 26, Forgery
Canyon County, 1948
Served 11 mos.

Pled guilty with her husband of cashing a forged check. The couple claimed to have committed the crime while intoxicated.

3115

BEATTIE, MARY
Age 24, Adultery
Madison County, 1922
Served 5 mos., 27 days

Charged after being caught in bed with a man who was not her husband. Beattie entered the ward pregnant and was released after giving birth to a son.

3919

BENOY, JEANNETTE
Age 65, Manslaughter
Idaho County, 1928
Served 2 yrs., 6 mos.

Convicted of shooting her husband in self-defense. A victim of frequent domestic abuse, Benoy shot her husband after he beat her with an iron bar.

5463

BESS, MARJORIE
Age 20, Robbery
Twin Falls County, 1937
Served 3 yrs., 5 mos., 20 days

Sent to prison after enticing a man into an alley where friends waited to rob him. After a conditional pardon, Bess was resentenced for prostitution.

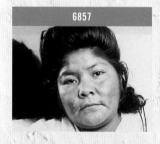

6857

BITT, ALICE WOFFIE
Age 21, Forgery
Elmore County, 1945
Served 4 mos., 9 days

Stole a blank check from a former employer. Bitt used the forged check to buy dresses and receive cash back at a Mountain Home store.

5497

BITTON, DOROTHY R.
Age 34, Obtaining Property Under False Pretenses
Ada County, 1937
Served 1 yr., 2 mos., 11 days

Arrested after writing a fake check. Hunted by the FBI, Bitton, a year after her release, returned to prison in Washington State.

■ VIOLENT CRIME ■ MORAL CRIME ■ THEFT CRIME ■ PETTY CRIME ■ OTHER CRIME

6071

BLACK, DAISY
Age 32, Burglary, Second Degree
Twin Falls County, 1939
Served 1 yr., 7 mos., 2 days

Robbed houses with her husband while passing through Idaho. A transient from Oklahoma, Black had a long criminal record dating back to age 13.

6090

BRDAR, CONSTANCE
Age 32, Grand Larceny
Clearwater County, 1940
Served 11 mos.

Stole a man's wallet and emptied it of cash and checks. Working as a waitress, Brdar went home with a stranger and proceeded to steal his money.

4694

BOGGAN, MARGUERITE
Age 34, Manslaughter, Involuntary
Lemhi County, 1932
Served 1 yr., 11 days

Convicted after fatally shooting her alcoholic husband. Boggan shot her husband at a brothel after he refused to go home with her.

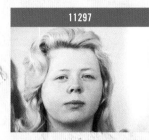

11297

BREZICKY, JANET ELAINE
Age 20, Robbery
Elmore County, 1963
Served 2 yrs., 1 day

Convicted of robbing the Royal Hotel in Mountain Home. Witnesses testified that Brezicky had cleaned out a cash register while holding clerks at gunpoint.

12326

BOISE, SHIRLEY ANN
Age 20, Assault With a Deadly Weapon
Bingham County, 1967
Served 11 mos., 25 days

Convicted for stabbing a woman in a drunken brawl. Resentenced for violating probation, Boise finished her sentence in the women's prison in Nevada.

5457

BROADHEAD, LELA
Age 36, Manslaughter, Involuntary
Power County, 1937
Served 1 yr., 3 mos., 30 days

Imprisoned for killing a 4-year-old, Georgia. Broadhead helped rear eight children, including Georgia, who was routinely beaten and abused.

3534

BOWMAN, EVA
Age 39, Inducing Girl to Enter Prostitution House
Ada County, 1925
Served 2 yrs.

Convicted with her husband of bootlegging during Prohibition. Bowman was also charged, but eventually acquitted, of recruiting women to work as prostitutes.

10251

BRONCHEAU, LAURA MARIE
Age 19, Grand Larceny
Nez Perce County, 1959
Served 10 mos., 19 days

Convicted of stealing two cars in the same night. Sentenced while pregnant, released to give birth, Broncheau finished the last six months of her sentence.

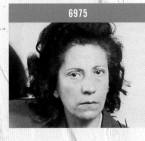

6975

BRADLEY, SARAH
Age 37, Forgery
Bannock County, 1946
Served 11 mos.

Convicted for forging checks in Pocatello. The mother of four young children, alone and desperate, Bradley promised to make restitution.

4238

BROOKS, AGNES
Age 37, Manslaughter, Involuntary
Bannock County, 1930
Served 8 mos.

Sentenced for reckless driving that killed a young man in his car. Brooks had sped through a stop sign, smashed a sedan, and ejected its driver.

Judy Louise Apnis lived a hard life. She attempted twice to commit suicide, once by turning on a gas stove.

3834

BROOKS, MARGARET
Age 20, Manslaughter
Bonner County, 1927
Served 1 yr., 1 mo., 26 days

Arrested for throwing her newborn baby from a train. Court documents alleged that Brooks suffered from a venereal disease affecting her state of mind.

2160

BROWN, GENEVA EMMA
Age 31, Assault With Intent to Commit Murder
Kootenai County, 1914
Served 1 yr., 9 mos.

Convicted of shooting a man and woman. Court documents noted Brown's tattoos, the first on record for Idaho's female inmates.

7121

BRYSON, BARBARA IRENE
Age 20, Grand Larceny
Bonneville County, 1947
Served 6 mos., 8 days

Convicted with a male accomplice of stealing $1,278. After six months on the run, Bryson turned herself in, claiming she feared for her life.

11532

BURRELL, BARBARA
Age 33, Issuing a Check Without Funds
Ada County, 1964
Served 1 yr., 1 mo.

Charged for violating probation and forging checks. An army veteran, Burrell had previously been arrested for disorderly conduct.

5302

BYBEE, ATHALIA
Age 23, Grand Larceny
Jerome County, 1936
Served 10 mos., 20 days

Indicted for stealing men's suits. Bybee and a female friend distracted retail clerks while their husbands made off with 24 suits.

5557

BYERS, VERNA SHIPLEY
Age 27, Exposing Person to Venereal Disease
Clearwater County, 1937
Served 7 mos., 22 days

Arrested with a male accomplice for exposing others to the disease. Born in Missouri, Byers ran afoul of the law in Montana before landing in the Idaho State Penitentiary.

12210

CALLOWAY, MARGARET E. PAXTON
Age 35, Insufficient Funds
Shoshone County, 1967
Served 11 mos.

Convicted for writing a check from an empty account. A Boisean, Calloway had previously been arrested for intoxication but had served no prison time.

3417

CARLTON, EDNA
Age 28, Conspiracy to Violate the Mann Act
U.S. Federal District Court, 1924
Served 1 yr., 3 days

Convicted for transporting women across state lines for the purpose of prostitution. Carlton and her husband took the women from Mountain Home to Seattle.

3044

CHACON, REBECCA
Age 31, Murder, Second Degree
Bannock County, 1921
Served 2 yrs., 3 mos., 8 days

Convicted with her husband of killing a former lover. A citizen of Mexico, Chacon was deported after serving her time.

2541

CHRISMAN, MARTHA
Age 29, Grand Larceny
Bingham County, 1917
Served 4 mos., 6 days

Prosecuted with two other women for stealing a car. Idaho's governor conditioned her pardon on Chrisman's pledge to return to family in Wyoming.

■ VIOLENT CRIME   ■ MORAL CRIME   ■ THEFT CRIME   ■ PETTY CRIME   ■ OTHER CRIME

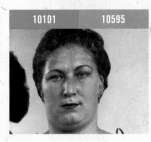

CHRISTOPHER, NANCY FRANCES
Age 26, Forgery, Escape
Gem County, 1958
Served 2 yrs., 5 mos.

Arrested for cashing a bad check at J.C. Penney in Emmett. Christopher, who wrote about daily life in the Women's Ward, was rearrested in Texas after she and two inmates climbed over the stone wall surrounding the ward.

CLARK, EVELINE
Age 23, Burglary, Second Degree
Bannock County, 1905
Served 3 yrs., 26 days

Served with a male accomplice; pled not guilty. Clark's release mandated monthly letters to the warden and abstinence from alcohol, narcotics, and gambling.

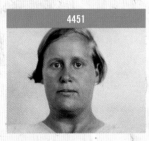

CLARK, HAZEL BELL
Age 32, Forgery
Bonneville County, 1931
Served 1 yr.

Forged several checks in Idaho Falls. Arrested previously for robbery and petty larceny, Clark was "clever in extracting money from her gentlemen friends."

COATS, KATHERINE MARIE
Age 21, Forgery
Twin Falls County, 1952
Served 11 mos., 6 days

Sentenced to 14 years for signing checks with her father's name. Coats's good behavior in prison secured her an early release and subsequent employment.

COCHRAN, SHARON LEE
Age 29, Burglary, First Degree
Twin Falls County, 1967
Served 2 yrs., 11 mos., 13 days

Convicted for robbing a Twin Falls Shell service station. On probation, Cochran violated her parole when she stabbed a 17-year-old boy fighting with her husband.

CONWAY, BESSIE
Age 25, Grand Larceny
Ada County, 1904
Served 11 mos.

Convicted of stealing a pocketbook and cash. Police found two $5 bills in Conway's mouth, which her defense lawyer claimed she had earned as a dressmaker.

COX, DOROTHY RUTH
Age 50, Issuing a Check Without Funds
Ada County, 1963
Served 1 yr., 7 mos., 29 days

Sentenced after passing several checks with insufficient funds in three states. Cox's closest companion was her son, who had epilepsy and cerebral palsy.

CRAIG, DOROTHY
Age 39, Forgery
Bannock County, 1959
Served 1 yr., 5 mos., 14 days

Charged in Idaho following a string of arrests in Louisiana and Washington. Craig entered prison expecting a child, but no record of the birth is known.

CRAWFORD, PHEDORA
Age 28, Assault With a Deadly Weapon
Lemhi County, 1898
Served 5 mos., 16 days

Arrested for her involvement in a beating and shooting. Crawford served time despite her unknown role in the assault; two men involved were not convicted.

CRUMROY, MARY
Age 44, Murder, Second Degree
Minidoka County, 1926
Served 14 yrs., 9 mos., 15 days

Charged with killing her husband after his exhumed body revealed arsenic. Crumroy moved to State Hospital South after setting fire to prison furniture.

Paul Newman starred in *Rally Round the Flag Boys!*, the Women's Ward's featured movie for October 1960.

SOURCE: WIKIMEDIA COMMONS

115

7222

CUNNINGHAM, ULETTA MAE
Age 20, Grand Larceny
Twin Falls County, 1947
Served 11 mos.

Arrested for stealing a purse and $100 from a Twin Falls department store. Homeless at age 13, Cunningham's first theft charge occurred in New Mexico.

4876

DEVANEY, MARJORY
Age 32, Assault With a Deadly Weapon
Blaine County, 1933
Served 4 mos., 18 days

Incarcerated after stabbing a man fighting with her husband. Devaney was pardoned after authorities received multiple letters of support.

1096

DALEY, JENNIE
Age 21, Manslaughter
Ada County, 1905
Served 6 yrs., 3 mos.

Sentenced to 10 years for the death of her husband. Daley first confessed, then claimed Fred Bond killed her husband out of love for her, and Bond was executed for the crime.

6939

DICK, MARGARET D.
Age 27, Forgery
Nez Perce County, 1946
Served 1 yr.

Arrested for forging an $80 check in Lewiston. Dick divorced her husband citing mental cruelty and spent her time in prison finding a home for her daughter.

1684

DAY, CLARA
Age 21, Assault With a Deadly Weapon
Bannock County, 1910
Served 1 yr., 3 mos., 8 days

Sentenced after attacking a Pocatello woman with a razor blade. Day wrote the parole board she was pregnant, although details of the birth are unknown.

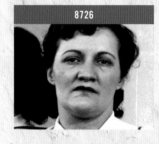

8726

DIRKS, MARGUERITE EVELYN
Age 34, Assault With a Deadly Weapon
Ada County, 1953
Served 1 yr., 3 mos., 15 days

Charged with stabbing her boyfriend with a kitchen knife. Prior arrests for disorderly conduct and drunkenness sent Dirks to the state hospital in Blackfoot.

12081

DEATON, BONNIE JEAN
Age 35, Manslaughter, Voluntary
Caribou County, 1966
Served 1 yr., 8 mos.

Imprisoned for shooting her husband. Deaton, claiming she never saw the gun or witnessed his death, attempted suicide by cutting her wrists before entering prison.

3056

DOUGLAS, HATTIE
Age 47, Grand Larceny
Jefferson County, 1921
Served 2 yrs., 3 mos., 11 days

Sentenced for stealing and reselling a black stallion in Idaho Falls. On parole, Douglas associated with cattle thieves, stole a car, and likely fled Idaho.

5341

DeCHEVERIEUX, JOY LOUISE
Age 17, Robbery
Bannock County, 1936
Served 1 yr., 1 mo., 13 days

Convicted of robbing $17 from a driver. DeCheverieux escaped with Marjorie Bess in 1937, but prison hounds found them two hours later in the foothills.

917

DUFFY, SUSIE
Age 17, Grand Larceny
Nez Perce County, 1903
Served 1 yr., 10 mos., 24 days

Arrested for robbing a man of $1,020. When Duffy was released, Boise's African American community bought her a train ticket to join family in Kansas City.

A man could be hanged for stealing a horse. Hattie Douglas of Jefferson County, convicted of stealing a stallion, served less than three years in the penitentiary.

■ VIOLENT CRIME ■ MORAL CRIME ■ THEFT CRIME ■ PETTY CRIME ■ OTHER CRIME

DUNN, CORA
Age 26, Obtaining Money Under False Pretenses
Twin Falls County, 1917
Served 1 yr., 10 mos., 2 days

Charged with passing fraudulent checks to purchase elegant furniture. Dunn claimed her recently deceased father left her a large sum of money.

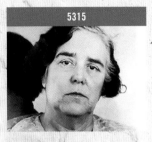

ECKERSLEY, EDNA L.
Age 53, Embezzlement by a Public Official
Lewis County, 1936
Served 4 yrs., 5 mos., 8 days

Convicted of stealing up to $40,000 while serving as Lewis County treasurer. Eckersley won two Western Idaho Fair ribbons for embroidery while incarcerated.

ELIASON, LEORA
Age 28, Adultery
Bannock County, 1942
Served 1 mo., 13 days

Arrested after her lover's children informed police. Eliason and her lover fled to Reno seeking annulment for him but were extradited to serve their sentences.

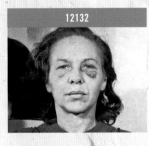

ELLIOTT, NAOMI ESTHER
Age 42, Forgery
Ada County, 1966
Served 10 mos., 25 days

Arrested after her daughter cashed checks forged by Elliott. After her husband's Utah forgery arrest, Elliott continued the practice to support their family.

ERICKSON, PATTI LOUISE
Age 24, Issuing Check Without Funds, Six Counts
Shoshone County, 1966
Served 11 mos.

Imprisoned for passing bad checks in three states. Erickson entered prison pregnant and gave birth in Boise; family cared for the child until her release.

ERNST, FRANCES
Age 26, Manslaughter
Valley County, 1919
Served 3 yrs., 7 mos., 16 days

Convicted of killing a neighbor after seeking divorce from her abusive husband. Ernst pulled the trigger, but her husband served time for handing her the gun.

FARR, MINNIE JANE
Age 57, Embezzlement
Kootenai County, 1944
Served 8 mos., 14 days

Imprisoned after stealing $9,000 as Kootenai County deputy treasurer. Although Farr lost the money gambling, over 200 citizens raised $9,000 in restitution.

FIELDS, MARGARET
Age 28, Grand Larceny
Bannock County, 1919
Served 4 mos., 25 days

Arrested for taking a purse left in a train car washroom. Prosecuting attorney suggested Fields's theft was understandable due to her gender and race.

FISHER, SADIE B.
Age 36, Manslaughter, Voluntary
Bannock County, 1948
Served 2 yrs., 15 days

Arrested for stabbing a man in the chest with a hunting knife during an argument about a dog. Fisher was pregnant when she began serving her sentence.

FOLDEN, HANNAH
Age 48, Violation of Prohibition Laws
Bonner County, 1923
Served 2 mos., 9 days

Imprisoned after two Prohibition-era arrests for concealing liquor in her home. Folden, labeled a "menace to society," was released to care for a war veteran.

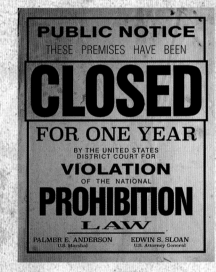

The sale of intoxicating liquors sent Hanna Folden to prison in 1923.

Industrial Pocatello was crime's gateway city for Josephine Fort and 24 other Women's Ward inmates.

SOURCE: JIMSAWTHAT, FLICKR

8407

FORT, JOSEPHINE
Age 34, Manslaughter, Involuntary
Bannock County, 1952
Served 3 yrs., 17 days

Arrested in Pocatello after killing her ex-husband. Arkansas-born Fort, while attempting to recover $35 owed to her, shot the man in self-defense.

6479

FOX, GRACE
Age 36, Forgery
Bannock County, 1941
Served 1 yr., 3 days

Charged with passing a $27 check in Pocatello. Fox and another prisoner later married and moved to Portland, where they ran a meat-packing business.

9465

GARDNER, HATTIE PEARL
Age 48, Forgery
Canyon County, 1956
Served 1 yr., 3 mos., 8 days

Charged with signing a check in her ex-husband's name. Gardner married in Oklahoma, where police arrested her 50 times for vagrancy, narcotics, and sex work.

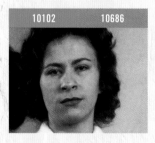

10102   **10686**

GARDNER, MARY ANN
Age 20, Forgery, Escape
Gem County, 1958
Served 2 yrs., 7 mo., 20 days

Imprisoned after passing fraudulent checks with four accomplices. One month after entering prison, Gardner escaped with Christopher and Pugmire, but her father promptly returned her to the prison.

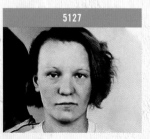

5127

GARLAND, BILLY
Age 23, Passing a Fictitious Check
Nez Perce County, 1935
Served 1 yr., 11 days

Arrested following a string of forged checks. Garland and Blackie Oliver, a pimp, traveled from Seattle to Lewiston, where they sold a stolen car.

10444

GEER, BARBARA ANN
Age 28, Obtaining Property Under False Pretenses
Bannock County, 1960
Served 1 yr., 1 mo., 12 days

Charged after buying a rifle and parka using her aunt's name. Geer was just 3 years old when her mother died and 14 when she married for the first time.

8337

GODDARD, KAY
Age 20, Burglary, First Degree
Twin Falls County, 1951
Served 1 yr., 4 mos., 11 days

Convicted after committing burglary in 19 states. Goddard served time only in Idaho; Wyoming police said, "We have more than enough of this class of people."

9556

GOINSALVOS, BARBARA ROSEMARY
Age 20, Forgery
Jerome County, 1956
Served 10 mos., 29 days

Charged with writing a bad check for $24.50 in Jerome. Goinsalvos and her husband had passed more than 100 fraudulent checks across the United States.

4321

GORDON, JUNE
Age 30, Passing a Fictitious Check
Twin Falls County, 1930
Served 1 yr.

Arrested for check forgery in the city of Filer. Gordon, the mother of eight, had also been arrested for exploiting her children through vagrancy and begging.

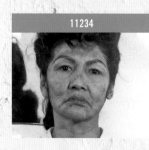

11234

GRANT, ELIZABETH LOVITA
Age 40, Forgery
Nez Perce County, 1963
Served 1 yr., 5 days

Convicted for the forging of checks. An orphan from the Nez Perce reservation, Grant suffered a troubled life of bad marriages and alcoholism.

■ VIOLENT CRIME   ■ MORAL CRIME   ■ THEFT CRIME   ■ PETTY CRIME   ■ OTHER CRIME

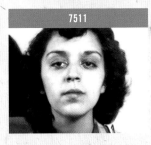

7511

GRANT, RUTH ANITA
Age 22, Forgery
Nez Perce County, 1948
Served 11 mos.

Convicted for forging checks. Grant described her crime as a mental breakdown in the aftermath of her husband's death, followed by the death of her son.

6731

HALFORD, RHODA T.
Age 23, Grand Larceny
Kootenai County, 1944
Served 6 mos., 24 days

Arrested in possession of stolen property, stashed away in a Coeur d'Alene cabin. A sympathetic parole officer kept Halford out of jail after a later arrest.

4693

HALL, HELEN
Age 34, Giving and Selling Liquor to a Minor
Lemhi County, 1932
Served 6 mos., 4 days

Convicted for bartering liquor to a boy of 19. In the city of Salmon, where she ran a notorious brothel, Hall was known for her orange-colored eyes.

6880

HAMMONS, EDNA G.
Age 21, Grand Larceny
Nez Perce County, 1945
Served 10 mos.

Arrested for lifting $275 from a man she seduced. Briefly incarcerated, Hammons reoffended in Washington (forgery) and Oregon (defrauding a taxi driver).

5304

HANSOM, MARY TURNER
Age 37, Manslaughter, Voluntary
Twin Falls County, 1936
Served 10 mos., 21 days

Convicted for killing in self-defense. Hansom, under assault from a vicious beating, shot her enraged fiancé.

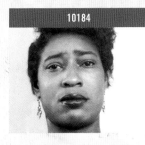

10184

HARAM, LUCILLE
Age 27, Manslaughter, Involuntary
Minidoka County, 1959
Served 2 yrs., 8 mos.

Convicted for murdering her common-law husband with a butcher knife in a public park in Rupert. Haram was paroled to Arizona after serving her sentence.

422

HARDY, MARGARET
Age 48, Murder, Second Degree
Latah County, 1895
Served 6 mos., 18 days

Convicted for killing her young daughter with morphine and carbolic acid. Hardy, after a short confinement, transferred to the state hospital for the insane.

12131

HARRISON, MILDRED LUCILLE
Age 38, Issuing a Check Without Funds
Nez Perce County, 1966
Served 1 yr.

Arrested in Lewiston for buying shoes with a fake name on an empty check. Harrison blamed her drunken husband for failing to fund the account.

11702

HARVEY, SHIRLEY ANN
Age 18, Issuing a Check Without Funds
Nez Perce County, 1965
Served 11 mos., 28 days

Arrested for writing a $10 check from an insufficient account. Harvey later confessed to writing three more bad checks while waiting on bail for trial.

2563

HARVILL, DORA
Age 48, Rape
Canyon County, 1917
Served 3 yrs., 6 mos.

Convicted for rape. Harvill looked away while her boyfriend bedded her teenage daughter. The boyfriend claimed the mother had given the daughter's consent.

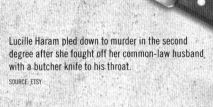

Lucille Haram pled down to murder in the second degree after she fought off her common-law husband with a butcher knife to his throat.

In 1945, on the Snake River's Lewiston-Clarkston Bridge, Edna Hammons lifted a leather wallet from a man's heavy overcoat. The wallet, minus $275, ended up in the river.

Edna Hester used a hot pan of lye to disfigure an abusive boyfriend. Paroled after serving two years, she was free only a month before fatally stabbing a woman in a barroom brawl.

2539

HATFIELD, MATILDA
Age 32, Grand Larceny
Bingham County, 1917
Served 4 mos., 7 days

Convicted with two other women of stealing an automobile. Police caught up with Hatfield and her companions in Utah, where they attempted to sell the car.

11717

HAYES, SUSAN ANN
Age 19, Manslaughter, Voluntary
Bannock County, 1965
Served 1 yr., 4 mos.

Convicted for her part in the murder of a Downey marshal. A male accomplice shot the marshal during a robbery while Hayes waited in the getaway car.

9877

HAYFORD, BERNA MAE
Age 29, Issuing a Check Without Funds
Twin Falls County, 1958
Served 10 mos., 23 days

Convicted for writing an empty check for $10 at a Twin Falls grocery store. Hayford and her husband admitted to writing more than a dozen fraudulent checks.

7272

HAYNES, RUTH
Age 31, Forgery
Twin Falls County, 1947
Served 11 mos., 1 day

Convicted for forging retail checks worth nearly $200. A Boisean, Hayes claimed she wrote the bad check to provide for a sickly husband and son.

5952

HAZELTINE, ALTA
Age 21, Robbery, Attempted
Latah County, 1939
Served 1 yr., 11 mos., 30 days

Convicted for attempt to commit robbery. Hazeltine and accomplice James Stephenson, also convicted, had attempted to con and rob a man in Moscow.

169

HENEBE
Age ?, Manslaughter
Bingham County, 1887
Served 1 yr., 12 days

Convicted for killing her husband on Fort Hall Reservation. Henebe was Idaho Territory's first and only female penitentiary inmate.

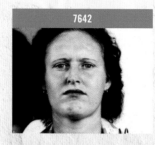

7642

HERRING, CLOREAN
Age 25, Forgery
Jefferson County, 1949
Served 11 mos., 28 days

Convicted for forging a $64 check at a Rigby Safeway. Herring, upon her release, married a former convict who had also served time at the penitentiary.

9202, 9718

HESTER, EDNA MAE
Age 37, Assault With Chemical; Manslaughter, Voluntary
Bannock County, 1955
Served 4 yrs., 7 mos., 26 days

Convicted for assault after dumping a pan of hot lye that disfigured her boyfriend and blinded him in one eye. In 1957, soon after serving her sentence, Hester returned to prison for manslaughter.

8109

HEWETT, LOLA GERTRUDE
Age 35, Issuing a Check Without Funds
Nez Perce County, 1950
Served 11 mos., 1 day

Convicted for insufficient funds after passing a $20 check in Lewiston. Hewett offered to repay but was charged after her husband beat the man she defrauded.

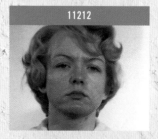

11212

HIGGINS, EUNICE ADA
Age 24, Issuing a No-Account Check
Canyon County, 1963
Served 11 mos.

Arrested after passing a $60 check at a Caldwell jewelry store. Higgins went to State Hospital South, escaped on Christmas Day, and was recaptured in Utah.

■ VIOLENT CRIME ■ MORAL CRIME ■ THEFT CRIME ■ PETTY CRIME ■ OTHER CRIME

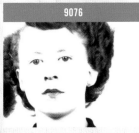

HINES, MARJORY LORAINE
Age 19, Issuing a Check Over $25 Without Funds
Owyhee County, 1954
Served 3 yrs., 4 days

Convicted for writing bad checks worth over $500 in two months. Hines violated parole for "sex delinquency" and leaving Idaho to marry a man in Nevada.

HOLMES, MARY
Age 46, Grand Larceny
Ada County, 1939
Served 11 mos., 20 days

Arrested after stealing a fur coat worth about $350 in Boise. Holmes's criminal career spanned 15 states with 13 different aliases.

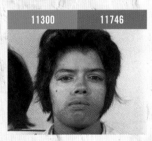

HOPKINS, MARY JANE
Age 22, Forgery, Grand Larceny
Bonneville County, 1963
Served 2 yrs., 8 mos., 4 days

Convicted for passing a check worth $34.27 at a market in Idaho Falls. On parole for just over a week, Hopkins was rearrested after stealing $380 out of a patient's wallet at a Boise nursing home.

HOPPER, ANGELA
Age 49, Embezzlement
Ada County, 1933
Served 2 yrs., 1 mo., 8 days

Convicted for pilfering $75,000 as a Boise City clerk. Hopper put the money into her son's account, resulting in his conviction for receiving stolen property.

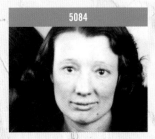

HUGHES, FERN
Age 32, Forgery
Gem County, 1935
Served 1 yr., 1 mo., 4 days

Convicted after passing two checks in Emmett totaling $45. Hughes claimed she was just trying to make ends meet for her three children.

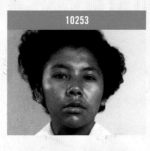

JABETH, ANNA MARIE
Age 20, Burglary, First Degree
Nez Perce County, 1959
Served 10 mos., 21 days

Convicted after her friends broke into a Lapwai shop and stole cigarettes, candy, potato chips, and soda. Jabeth remained in the car during the robbery.

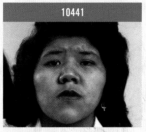

JABETH, JOSEPHINE
Age 19, Burglary in the Night Time, First Degree
Nez Perce County, 1960
Served 1 yr., 4 mos., 22 days

Charged with breaking into a business in Culdesac. Jabeth was 16 when she was sent to St. Anthony Industrial School after stealing a man's wallet and car.

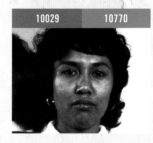

JAMES, LORRAINE SYLVIA
Age 19, Grand Larceny, Forgery
Nez Perce County, 1958
Served 2 yrs., 7 mos., 30 days

Convicted after robbing a Lewiston man at knifepoint with three other women. Later rearrested after passing a $62 check at a drugstore, James violated her parole by stealing a car with her common-law husband.

JOHNSON, JOEANNE
Age 28, Assault With a Deadly Weapon
Bonneville County, 1957
Served 1 yr.

Arrested with her common-law husband when a man was shot and robbed in an Idaho Falls motel. The victim claimed someone other than Johnson did the shooting.

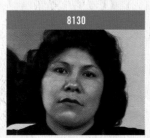

KAIYOU, CECILIA
Age 22, Burglary, Second Degree
Bingham County, 1950
Served 1 yr., 5 mos., 29 days

Charged with breaking into a Blackfoot home and stealing a radio and camera. Kaiyou said she was drunk at the time, hoping to pawn the items for intoxicants.

Boise police arrested Mary Holmes as she attempted to steal an expensive fur coat. By 1945, under 13 different names, she had committed crimes in at least 15 states.

SOURCE: INTERNATIONAL FUR STORE

121

Elizabeth Lacey's husband survived her first attempt to kill him with strychnine. Lacey succeeded at last by lacing the bottle of whiskey he kept in his car.

7282

KELLER, VERNA BELLA
Age 17, Murder, Second Degree
Bonner County, 1947
Served 7 yrs., 8 mos.

Convicted with her boyfriend of killing a 16-year-old girl she thought was too flirtatious. With a makeshift ladder, Keller escaped prison but was recaptured.

6807

KENDRICK, DOROTHY H.
Age 19, Robbery
Twin Falls County, 1945
Served 2 yrs., 3 mos., 24 days

Convicted with her boyfriend after a spree of robberies ended in Twin Falls. Kendrick and her boyfriend were found by a janitor they had beaten and robbed.

565

KENSLER, JOSIE
Age 25, Murder, Second Degree
Elmore County, 1897
Served 12 yrs., 6 mos., 2 days

Convicted with her lover of killing her husband. Kensler later claimed a guard impregnated her and the warden and physician forced her to have an abortion.

8410

KIDD, LULA MAE
Age 20, Forgery, Issuing a Check Without Funds
Cassia County, 1952
Served 9 mos., 2 days

Arrested after passing a $5 check at a Burley ice cream shop. Kidd, who claimed she was drunk and didn't recall the crime, gave birth to a child in prison.

11513

KING, LALONDA LEE
Age 19, Robbery
Nez Perce County, 1964
Served 1 yr., 10 mos., 2 days

Convicted after stealing an elderly woman's purse in Lewiston. King, who preferred the nickname "Tim," claimed friends coaxed her to commit the crime.

8600

KLINGENSMITH, MARY MARGARET
Age 33, Issuing a Check Without Funds
Ada County, 1953
Served 10 mos., 20 days

Arrested after writing a $10 check at the M&W Market in Boise. Klingensmith had asked the proprietor to keep the check until she returned to pay with cash.

8676

KNOX, MILDRED LOUISE
Age 28, Grand Larceny
Twin Falls County, 1953
Served 6 mos., 27 days

Convicted after admitting she took a man's wallet containing $4,220 at a bar in Kimberly for "safekeeping." A vocalist, Knox sang cowboy and western ballads.

2315

KOLB, HATTIE
Age 23, Adultery
Kootenai County, 1915
Served 1 yr., 2 days

Arrested when found living "in sin" in a Coeur d'Alene boarding house. Kolb's husband received a divorce but offered to remarry for their children's sake.

7610

LACEY, ELIZABETH LOTTIE
Age 37, Murder, First Degree
Canyon County, 1949
Served 13 yrs., 7 mos., 29 days

Convicted after poisoning her abusive ex-husband with strychnine-laced whiskey in Homedale. Lacey had a scar on her neck from his attempt to slit her throat.

901

LAHERTY, IDA
Age 16, Grand Larceny
Latah County, 1903
Served 3 mos., 1 day

Convicted after hiring a team of horses in Moscow and attempting to sell them in Washington. Laherty was released early due to concern over her young age.

■ VIOLENT CRIME   ■ MORAL CRIME   ■ THEFT CRIME   ■ PETTY CRIME   ■ OTHER CRIME

5949

LANG, DELLA
Age 22, Attempt to Commit Forgery
Cassia County, 1939
Served 1 yr., 6 mos., 13 days

Sentenced for an attempt to cash a check in Burley signed with the name of a "prominent sheepman." Both Lang and her boyfriend served time for forgery.

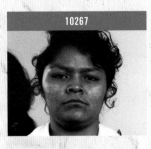

10267

LAWYER, CARON SPENCER
Age 18, Burglary, First Degree
Nez Perce County, 1959
Served 1 yr., 10 mos., 18 days

Arrested after friends broke into a Lapwai shop and stole cigarettes, candy, potato chips, and soda. Lawyer helped carry the stolen goods out of the store.

11915

LEE, ROSETTA
Age 34, Issuing Check Without Funds, Two Counts
Minidoka County, 1965
Served 11 mos.

Convicted for insufficient funds after passing two $25 checks at the Ponderosa Inn in Burley. Lee turned herself over to the sheriff.

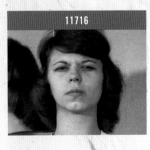

11716

LEHIY, FRANCIS
Age 27, Manslaughter, Voluntary
Bannock County, 1965
Served 1 yr., 8 mos., 20 days

Arrested after burglars she operated with killed the Downey marshal during an attempted robbery. Lehiy claimed she was asleep in the car during the attack.

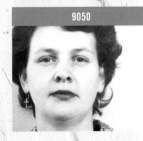

9050

LENNON, ELDA LEE
Age 25, Forgery
Ada County, 1954
Served 1 yr., 5 mos., 18 days

Convicted after passing five checks worth $30 each in Boise grocery stores. Authorities suspected Lennon's husband had forced her to pass the checks.

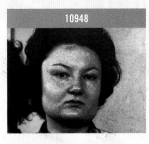

10948

LOFTIS, RAMONA JO
Age 18, Arson, Second Degree
Shoshone County, 1962
Served 11 mos., 16 days

Sentenced after setting fire to her detention cell in the Shoshone County Hospital. Loftis's first detention occurred when she ran away from home at age 13.

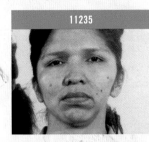

11235

LOPEZ, CLAIRE JOHNSON
Age 32, Forgery
Nez Perce County, 1963
Served 1 yr., 7 mos., 2 days

Convicted after passing a bad check. After breaking rules in the Women's Ward, Lopez was sent to the Ada County Jail "for security reasons."

8939

LOVELACE, VIRGINIA MARIE
Age 28, Forgery
Canyon County, 1954
Served 1 yr., 4 mos., 22 days

Convicted after passing a $68.85 check near Caldwell with her husband. Caught in Montana, the Lovelaces had passed nearly $600 worth of bad checks in Idaho.

4345

LOWE, VIOLA
Age 25, Forgery
Twin Falls County, 1931
Served 11 mos.

Served for stealing funds from the Twin Falls County Superintendent of Public Instruction while acting as clerk. Lowe vehemently maintained her innocence.

11767

LYLE, ANNA FAYE
Age 21, Issuing a Check Without Funds
Ada County, 1965
Served 9 mos., 27 days

Convicted of writing several worthless checks in Boise. Lyle earned her GED in prison and was "ambitious, self-motivated, and determined" upon parole.

The Idaho State Industrial School in St. Anthony, a girls reformatory, opened in 1924. Caron Lawyer was one of many alumni who graduated into burglary and other crimes.
SOURCE: ISHS

Lipstick on the collar of Virginia Mahoney's boyfriend had allegedly ignited the quarrel that left him dead and sent her to prison for manslaughter.

11739

MAHONEY, VIRGINIA MAXINE
Age 24, Manslaughter, Involuntary
Kootenai County, 1965
Served 2 yrs., 4 mos.

Served time for killing her allegedly abusive husband. In one story version, Mahoney said lipstick on his collar initiated the fight that led to his death.

8568

McCULLUM, ZONA
Age 40, Assault With a Deadly Weapon
Twin Falls County, 1953
Served 11 mos.

Convicted for stabbing her common-law husband in the chest at a bar in Twin Falls. McCullum, a habitual drinker, told police "everything went black."

11299

MANNING, MARILYN FAYE
Age 19, Forgery
Ada County, 1963
Served 1 yr., 10 mos., 25 days

Convicted for writing 27 worthless checks totaling $439.10. Four months into her sentence, Manning gave birth to a baby girl at Saint Alphonsus Hospital.

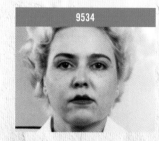

9534

McDONALD, DOROTHY LEE
Age 34, Forgery
Twin Falls County, 1956
Served 1 yr.

Found guilty of forging checks totaling $1,000. McDonald's habitual criminal activity spanned at least six states, from Colorado to California.

11581

McCONVILLE, JUDITH ANNE
Age 18, Burglary in the Night Time
Nez Perce County, 1964
Served 2 yrs., 1 mo., 4 days

Convicted for stealing typewriters, a movie projector, and a briefcase from Lewiston High School. McConville obtained leave to attend her father's funeral.

1464

McGEE, ALTA
Age 36, Assault With a Deadly Weapon
Ada County, 1908
Served 3 mos., 2 days

Convicted for shooting at her estranged husband in downtown Boise. McGee, the prosecutor argued, retaliated against her husband for flaunting other women.

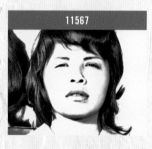

11567

McCONVILLE, MARY LUCY
Age 22, Burglary in the Night Time
Nez Perce County, 1964
Served 8 mos., 19 days

Served time for her role in the theft of $25 worth of equipment from Lewiston High School. While in prison, McConville corresponded with a U.S. Army private.

11841

McLAWS, EMILY MAY
Age 30, False Use of Credit Card to Obtain Goods
Twin Falls County, 1965
Served 2 yrs., 5 mos., 27 days

Imprisoned for using stolen checks and credit cards. McLaws suffered from narcolepsy and perhaps other unknown mental illnesses.

1537

McCORMICK, HATTIE
Age 29, Adultery
Washington County, 1909
Served 4 mos., 12 days

Convicted for having an affair. Although McCormick and her partner claimed to be estranged from their spouses, both pled guilty to charges of adultery.

6792

McWILLIAMS, ARLENE
Age 18, Burglary, First Degree
Kootenai County, 1944
Served 11 mos.

Served time for her role in a Coeur d'Alene burglary. Released to live with her father, McWilliams stayed out of trouble, married, and moved to Louisiana.

■ VIOLENT CRIME　■ MORAL CRIME　■ THEFT CRIME　■ PETTY CRIME　■ OTHER CRIME

11892

MILLER, LOUISE ALICE
Age 52, Forgery
Shoshone County, 1965
Served 3 yrs., 10 mos., 2 days

Convicted for forging a $20 check in Wallace. A month after her conviction, Miller was granted a two-week reprieve to attend her husband's funeral.

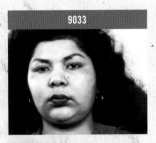

9033

MILLER, PHYLLIS MAE
Age 23, Manslaughter, Voluntary
Clearwater County, 1954
Served 4 yrs., 3 mos., 20 days

Imprisoned for stabbing a man in the heart in a brawl. Conditionally released, Miller violated parole when she assaulted a neighbor.

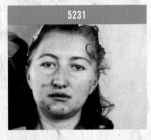

5231

MILLS, MARY J.
Age 20, Exposing a Person to a Dangerous Disease
Ada County, 1935
Served 11 mos.

Convicted for spreading a venereal disease. Prosecutors alleged that Mills had been living with "men of low moral character."

11630

MINK, PHYLLIS MAE
Age 26, No-Account Check
Bingham County, 1964
Served 1 yr., 26 days

Convicted for writing a $50 fraudulent check. Having survived the recent death of her husband and two children, Mink suffered from alcoholism.

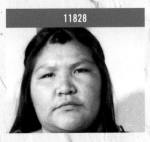

11828

MONCISCO, PHILNOMA MAXINE
Age 24, Robbery
Bingham County, 1965
Served 1 yr., 5 mos., 29 days

Convicted with an accomplice for stealing a wallet from a tavern in Blackfoot. A year before, Moncisco's brother had murdered her husband.

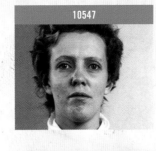

10547

MONTGOMERY, KAY ELAINE
Age 23, Forgery
Bannock County, 1960
Served 2 yrs., 8 mos., 20 days

Sentenced for forging checks in a crime spree across several states. Montgomery claimed her life on the lam began as a means to escape her abusive husband.

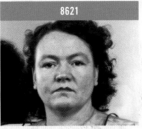

8621

MOORE, PATRICIA JUANITA
Age 36, Issuing Checks Without Sufficient Funds
Washington County, 1953
Served 11 mos., 4 days

Incarcerated for writing a $50 fraudulent check. Moore's previous four-state criminal record included embezzlement, vagrancy, and prostitution.

3955

MUGUERZA, ELLA
Age 21, Assault With a Deadly Weapon
Cassia County, 1928
Served 1 yr., 3 mos., 9 days

Convicted for shooting her husband. At trial Muguerza claimed that a pistol accidentally fired during an altercation over spoiled meat.

3117

NEIBAUR, ALICE
Age 50, Adultery
Madison County, 1922
Served 1 yr., 7 days

Convicted for sex with a man other than her husband. Neibaur's husband had been serving penitentiary time for the sexual assault of a 7-year-old girl.

5149

NEWALL, IDA
Age 27, Forgery
Bannock County, 1935
Served 11 mos., 16 days

Convicted with her husband for writing bad checks at J.C. Penney in Pocatello. Prison intake papers noted the "dope scars" of morphine addiction.

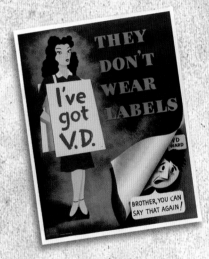

Mary Mills and Mildred Wilcox were among the many Idaho inmates with syphilis or gonorrhea. Public hygiene posters blamed women for sexually transmitted diseases.

SOURCE: REDDIT

Leola Norris, in 1931, became the first of many Women's Ward inmates to have colored hair noted on her intake form. The color was called "drugstore red."

SOURCE: VINTAGEADBROWSER.COM

9038

NICKOLAUSON, MARGARET JEAN
Age 52, Burglary
Boundary County, 1954
Served 10 mos., 22 days

Found guilty of stealing shirts from a J.C. Penney store in Bonner's Ferry. A native of Ireland, Nickolauson was released to immigration authorities.

4486

NORRIS, LEOLA
Age 25, Adultery
Clearwater County, 1931
Served 6 mos., 22 days

Convicted for sex with a married man who was not her husband. Prison intake papers noted Norris's dyed hair, calling it "drugstore red."

9423

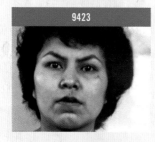

OATMAN, BEULAH SHIRLEY
Age 25, Robbery
Nez Perce County, 1956
Served 1 yr., 8 mos.

Convicted, with two male accomplices, for robbery. Released on probation, Oatman was again indicted and sentenced for fighting and intoxication.

11415

OLIVER, GLORIA JEAN
Age 18, Forgery
Clearwater County, 1963
Served 2 yrs., 4 mos.

Convicted for forging checks and again for violating probation. After her second conviction, she faithfully attended a prison program for alcoholics.

11885

ORTH, LOIS ADA
Age 35, Issuing an Insufficient Funds Check
Bonneville County, 1965
Served 1 yr.

Convicted for overdrafting a series of fraudulent checks. At trial, Orth blamed the crime spree on apathy induced by bad medication.

2540

PAPPAS, ELLEN
Age 21, Grand Larceny
Bingham County, 1917
Served 4 mos., 6 days

Convicted with four accomplices for stealing a car. An immigrant from Scotland, Pappas was required to leave Idaho as a condition of her parole.

6626

PARSLEY, DAISY ELIZABETH HIMM
Age 16, Bigamy
Nez Perce County, 1943
Served 11 mos., 2 days

Convicted for marrying a second husband without properly divorcing the first. A judge required Parsley to get legally married as a condition of her parole.

9721

PAUL, ERNESTINE WANDA
Age 20, Grand Larceny
Served 1 yr., 6 mos.

Pled guilty to robbing a man at knifepoint. Paul and accomplices, having hitched a ride, stole the driver's wallet and car.

10233, 10620

PAUL, INA JANE
Age 33, Forgery
Lewis County, 1959
Served 2 yrs., 6 mos., 22 days

Convicted after a series of arrests for vagrancy and check fraud. A Nez Perce tribal member, Paul was released after a court stated Idaho could not prosecute crimes committed on Indian reservations.

9647

PEO, MARIE REUBEN
Age 19, Burglary, First Degree
Bingham County, 1957
Served 11 mos.

Convicted with accomplices for stealing from a building owned by a church in Blackfoot. Witnesses testified that Peo had waited outside during the theft.

■ VIOLENT CRIME ■ MORAL CRIME ■ THEFT CRIME ■ PETTY CRIME ■ OTHER CRIME

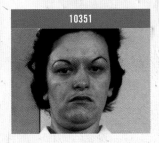

10351

PETERSON, DONNA MAE
Age 25, Burglary, First Degree
Canyon County, 1959
Served 10 mos., 22 days

Convicted with a male accomplice for stealing narcotics. After violating probation, Peterson entered a rehab program for alcoholics.

7035

PETERSON, ETHELYN IRENE
Age 32, Murder, Second Degree
Canyon County, 1946
Served 3 yrs.

Sentenced for banging her 3-year-old stepson's head against a bridge. Enraged by the boy's bedwetting, Peterson claimed medication altered her personality.

6325

PHILLIPS, FLOSSIE
Age 19, Manslaughter, Voluntary
Lincoln County, 1941
Served 5 mos., 7 days

Imprisoned for her role in her father's death. Phillips and her brothers said years of abuse led to their plot to scare and harm but not kill him.

8760

PROUD, LENA PINK
Age 65, Procurement of Abortion
Owyhee County, 1953
Served 10 mos., 29 days

Sentenced for providing an abortion to an unwed woman. Before prison, Proud gave astrological readings and helped women find homes for their newborn babies.

9216, 10587

PUGMIRE, VIRGINIA LORENE
Age 19, Forgery
Bannock County, 1955
Served 4 yrs., 7 mos., 7 days

Arrested for passing a bad check in Pocatello. After fleeing the prison with two other inmates, "Pug" knocked on the door of a Boise homeowner asking to call a taxi because her car had broken down.

7071

RANDOLPH, DOROTHY ILENE
Age 24, Grand Larceny
Nez Perce County, 1946
Served 7 mos., 13 days

Incarcerated for stealing items from a man who died after an altercation with her husband's friend. Randolph eventually settled in La Grande, Oregon.

8451

REASONER, CLAIRE
Age 24, Forgery
Twin Falls County, 1952
Served 11 mos., 1 day

Imprisoned for writing checks in her boss's name in Buhl. Reasoner worked as a hotel manager after her release from prison.

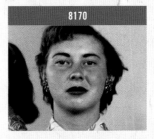

8170

REEMS, ALWILDA VERNEMARY
Age 15, Murder, Second Degree
Lincoln County, 1951
Served 5 yrs., 7 mos., 1 day

Convicted for assisting her boyfriend in the shooting death of her father. Reems claimed her father had repeatedly sexually abused her.

4587

RHYMER, GENEVIEVE H.
Age 20, Forgery
Gem County, 1932
Served 9 mos.

Committed forgery in Emmett. According to an *Idaho Statesman* article, Rhymer and inmate Lyda Southard attended church services together at the prison.

11861

ROACH, SARAH SUE
Age 55, Prostitution
Cassia County, 1965
Served 2 yrs., 5 mos.

Convicted for acting as a "madame" and taking the earnings of a prostitute. Before her conviction, Roach ran for Burley mayor and received 1% of the vote.

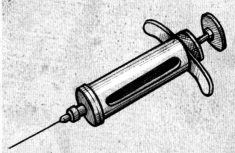

Donna Peterson was one of many female inmates addicted to narcotics. Today, nationwide, drugs and alcohol are listed as contributing factors in more than half of female felony crimes.

ROGERS, JO ANN
Age 44, Obtaining Money Under False Pretenses
Ada County, 1954
Served 1 yr., 2 mos., 13 days

Sentenced for bilking $1,500 from a friend under the guise of "investment." While in prison, Rogers attempted to sue former neighbors in Los Angeles.

8792

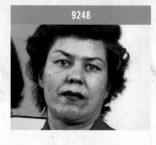

SANDERS, FRANCES
Age 32, Injury to Bannock County Jail
Bannock County, 1955
Served 6 mos., 6 days

Convicted of sawing through the steel bars of her county jail cell. Sanders's original sentence was for stealing a dress with a forged check.

9248

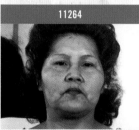

ROGERS, KATHLEEN STONE
Age 37, Grand Larceny
Bingham County, 1963
Served 1 yr., 3 mos.

Sentenced after stealing $40 worth of coins from a laundromat. Arrested over 30 times for charges related to drunkenness, Rogers suffered from alcoholism.

11264

SCHAEFFER, ELIZABETH LYNNE
Age 25, Assault With Deadly Weapon, Resisting Officers
Kootenai County, 1968
Served 8 mos., 29 days

Convicted for assault after a gun battle with police at a Coeur d'Alene motel. Schaeffer also served time for narcotics.

12365

ROOTS, GLADYS
Age 19, Forgery
Jerome County, 1931
Served 5 mos., 19 days

Imprisoned for forging two checks in Jerome. Roots claimed she alone committed the crime, but officials believed her husband participated.

4356

SCHRAEDER, ROBERTA BLANCHE
Age 35, Issuing an Insufficient Funds Check Over $25
Ada County, 1964
Served 4 mos., 8 days

Convicted of writing checks on an empty account. Schraeder claimed she was drawn to Idaho because it was "an easy area to pass paper."

11667

ROSS, MAMIE
Age 39, Receiving Stolen Property
Cassia County, 1916
Served 5 days

Incarcerated for possessing items she knew had been stolen. Ross, who lived in squalor with eight children, was let go early to tend to her 2-week-old baby.

2404

SCOTT, GRACE ELIZABETH
Age 53, Manslaughter, Involuntary
Boise County, 1951
Served 2 yrs., 24 days

Convicted of a hit-and-run that left a motorist dead in Horseshoe Bend. Scott had veered off the road, crushing a man who had stopped to fix his car.

8151

SAMPLEY, CORA
Age 42, Manslaughter, Involuntary
Nez Perce County, 1923
Served 1 yr., 6 mos., 26 days

Convicted for killing a young woman in a botched abortion. Prosecutors claimed Sampley and her accomplice, a barber, were "habitual" abortion providers.

3231

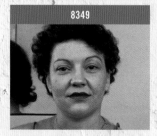

SEKINGER, RUTH ELLEN
Age 32, Assault With Intent to Commit Robbery
Ada County, 1951
Served 2 yrs., 1 mo., 2 days

Convicted for driving the getaway car in a botched robbery turned fatal. Sekinger's accomplice had fired on a grocery clerk chasing them with a meat cleaver.

8349

Alcoholism rose with the drinking ads that targeted women. Inmates like Kathleen Rogers suffered the tragic effects.

ALBERT FISHER, POSTER MUSEUM

■ VIOLENT CRIME   ■ MORAL CRIME   ■ THEFT CRIME   ■ PETTY CRIME   ■ OTHER CRIME

11389

SHIELDS, DARLENE MAE
Age 32, Grand Larceny
Ada County, 1963
Served 11 mos., 3 days

Convicted of grabbing cash from an open till at a Boise Albertsons Market. On probation, Shields was convicted again for brandishing a knife in a bar brawl.

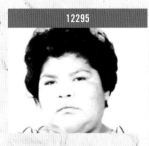

12295

SHORT, ROSEANNE
Age 25, Assault With a Deadly Weapon
Bingham County, 1967
Served 1 yr., 3 days

Convicted of assault under circumstances that have faded from the public record. Short may have been a Shoshone-Bannock Indian from the Fort Hall Reservation.

11732

SHREVE, LULA ANN
Age 43, Manslaughter, Involuntary
Shoshone County, 1965
Served 3 yrs.

Convicted for abusing and killing her 4-year-old foster child. Shreve's child died in a basement with chain bruises around her neck.

1146

SHUPE, CADDIE
Age 36, Manslaughter, Voluntary
Bear Lake County, 1905
Served 3 yrs., 1 mo., 1 day

Convicted of shooting her lover while the man was bathing. Shupe said it was suicide, but forensics showed the shooter was standing above the victim's chest.

9420

SIMMONS, CLARE SAVANNA
Age 30, Issuing a Check Without Funds
Kootenai County, 1956
Served 9 mos., 8 days

Convicted for her part in a husband-wife multistate check-writing spree. In prison, Simmons, a mother of four, broke some ribs when she fell off the top bunk.

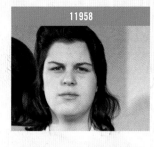

11958

SIMPSON, KAREN LEE
Age 19, Issuing a No-Account Check
Bonneville County, 1966
Served 11 mos.

Convicted of writing bad checks in Washington, Idaho, and Montana. The crime spree began when Simpson took up with a notorious burglar.

8918, 10065, 11196, 11848

SINGLETON, BARBARA ANN
Age 24, Issuing Checks Without Funds
Madison County, 1954
Served 6 yrs., 1 mo., 28 days

Convicted and sentenced on four different occasions for papering Twin Falls with "no account" checks. Singleton "evidently enjoyed writing checks," said the deadpan prosecutor.

8446

SKINNER, JUNE LAVON
Age 21, Forgery
Twin Falls County, 1952
Served 11 mos.

Convicted after a drunken check-bouncing bender in Wells, Nevada. Skinner's crimes included parole violations for cohabitation with an ex-convict.

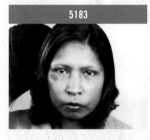

5183

SMITH, DELIA
Age 24, Robbery
Nez Perce County, 1935
Served 1 yr., 9 mos., 5 days

Convicted with a male accomplice of hijacking a car at gunpoint. Smith had "criminal tendencies" and "a hard attitude toward society," prosecutors said.

8668

SMITH, FRANCES IRENE
Age 22, Burglary
Bannock County, 1953
Served 1 yr., 1 mo., 6 days

Convicted with a male accomplice of burglarizing a home in Pocatello. Smith was also wanted for burglaries in Missouri.

Repeat Offenders

Nancy Frances Christopher
(2) Forgery, Escape

Mary Ann Gardner (2)
Forgery, Escape

Edna Mae Hester (2)
Assault With a Chemical, Manslaughter

Mary Jane Hopkins (2)
Forgery, Grand Larceny

Lorraine Sylvia James (2)
Forgery, Grand Larceny

Ina Jane Paul (2) Forgery

Virginia Lorene Pugmire (2)
Forgery, Escape

Barbara Ann Singleton (4)
Issuing a Check Without Funds

Shirley Ann Spencer and four other girls asked a man to give them a ride home. He agreed and three miles outside of Lapwai, one of the girls stuck a knife in the back of the man's neck and told him to pull over. Though he struggled against them, the group was able to overpower him, stealing his wallet and the car.

1692 — SMITH, MARY
Age 33, Adultery
Washington County, 1910
Served 3 mos., 3 days

Convicted of "infidelity to her husband." Arrested near Weiser, Smith pled for clemency due to poor health and the need to care for her children.

3052 — SOUTHARD, LYDA
Age 29, Murder, Second Degree
Twin Falls County, 1921
Served 18 yrs., 7 mos., 23 days

Convicted of poisoning her husband. Prosecutors produced evidence that Southard, dubbed "Lady Bluebeard," had murdered four husbands and a stepdaughter.

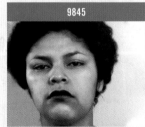

9845 — SPENCER, SHIRLEY ANN
Age 21, Grand Larceny
Nez Perce County, 1958
Served 11 mos., 28 days

Convicted for hijacking a car with a knife. Spencer was released after a court ruled that Idaho had no jurisdiction to prosecute crimes on Indian reservations.

1482 — STANFIELD, CORA
Age 36, Adultery
Canyon County, 1908
Served 5 mos., 11 days

Convicted with a male accomplice in Nampa "for living as man and wife." Stanfield's estranged husband had tracked her down while searching for his daughter.

11795 — STARR, FREDA MAE
Age 29, Forgery
Bingham County, 1965
Served 1 yr., 5 mos., 16 days

Convicted with husband for forging checks. Starr's crimes also included stealing a car in West Virginia, child abuse, and statutory rape.

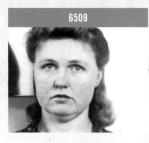

6509 — STARR, HAZEL IRENE
Age 27, Forgery
Twin Falls County, 1942
Served 8 mos.

Convicted with husband of forging names on checks. Starr's parole board recommended she stay away from beer and beer parlors.

11258 — TANNER, JOYCE A. BROWN
Age 34, Forgery
Nez Perce County, 1963
Served 10 mos., 17 days

Convicted for check fraud at a Lewiston bar. Bad checks also sent Tanner's husband to prison in three western states.

9533 — TATE, DOROTHY JEAN
Age 31, Forgery
Nez Perce County, 1956
Served 10 mos., 19 days

Convicted of purchasing a $25 bus ticket with a forged check. Placed on probation, Tate was rearrested for changing her address without notifying the court.

3267 — THOMPSON, IRENE
Age 38, Adultery
Cassia County, 1923
Served 7 mos., 8 days

Convicted for cohabiting with a married man in Burley. Prosecutors also charged Thompson of the abusive neglect of her four youngest children.

7695 — TURNER, ELOISE M.
Age 22, Forgery
Jerome County, 1949
Served 8 mos.

Convicted of a pharmaceutical check-cashing swindle in Idaho and Utah. At times Turner sold the con by pretending to be pregnant or dressing up as a nurse.

■ VIOLENT CRIME   ■ MORAL CRIME   ■ THEFT CRIME   ■ PETTY CRIME   ■ OTHER CRIME

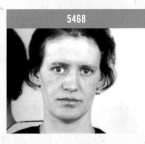

5468

TWITCHELL, THELMA
Age 27, Forgery
Cassia County, 1937
Served 1 yr., 1 mo., 5 days

Convicted of forging a series of checks for sums as small as $5. Confined to her cell for "insolence," Twitchell died young, possibly from alcohol-related issues.

2326

UNDERWOOD, DOLLIE
Age 32, Robbery
Bonner County, 1915
Served 1 yr., 7 mos.

Convicted with her male accomplice of hijacking a car at gunpoint. Often alone in her cellblock, Underwood sewed cushions for chairs.

600

VAN LUVEN, MARY
Age 33, Assault With a Deadly Weapon
Lemhi County, 1897
Served 1 yr., 8 mos., 29 days

Convicted of shooting her landlady in a rent dispute. Trial reporters noted Van Luven's forlorn, almost "inhuman" appearance.

7954

VAN OSTRAND, NORMA
Age 30, Embezzlement
Cassia County, 1950
Served 10 mos., 24 days

Convicted of embezzling payroll from a grain supply company in Burley. Apprehended in Reno, Van Ostrand was arrested with a male felon, her fiancé.

5303

VANCE, ELLEN
Age 27, Grand Larceny
Jerome County, 1936
Served 10 mos., 20 days

Convicted with three accomplices of stealing men's suits from a retail store. Prosecutors alleged that Vance distracted a clerk while the men stole suits.

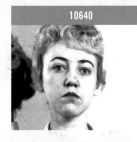

10640

VEST, CHERIE KAYE
Age 19, Forgery
Bonneville County, 1960
Served 1 yr., 3 mos.

Convicted of forging checks and breaking parole. A teenage runaway, Vest spent time in hospitals and reformatories, accused of "homosexual acts."

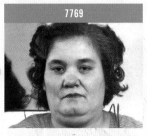

7769

WEBB, FRANCES
Age 43, Forgery
Ada County, 1949
Served 1 yr., 3 mos., 16 days

Convicted of disturbing the peace, unlawful cohabitation, and forgery. An abused child and widowed twice, Webb claimed to have been tricked into crimes while drugged.

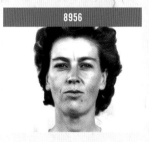

8956

WEISE, JEAN FULLMER
Age 27, Manslaughter, Involuntary
Kootenai County, 1954
Served 1 yr.

Convicted after a deadly crash on an Idaho highway. The court commuted Weise's 14-year sentence after she had served only a year.

8975

WELLS, REEDA COLLEEN
Age 18, Grand Larceny
Bonneville County, 1954
Served 10 mos., 26 days

Convicted for breaking into and stealing from cars. Wells violated parole when she left the state of Idaho without notifying her probation officer.

3234

WILCOX, MILDRED
Age 23, Forgery
Canyon County, 1923
Served 1 yr., 1 mo., 12 days

Convicted for her part in what prosecutors called a "certified check racket." Pregnant in prison, Wilcox was sent to Boise's Salvation Army to give birth.

Dion's "Lonely Teenager" was an aptly named hit with inmate Cherie Vest, herself a lonely teenager, who listed the song as a fav in *The Clock*.

SOURCE: DISCOGS

Terror flashed through the logging town of Wallace when Anna and Richard Woodfine, hoping for insurance money, set their small home on fire. Eight years earlier, an inferno of historic proportions had devastated timber country.

3333

WILSON, ALICE
Age 42, Forgery
Ada County, 1923
Served 1 yr., 2 mos., 19 days

Convicted of cashing a forged check at the Boise City National Bank. A nurse, she ran a home for unwed mothers. Charges of performing an illegal abortion were dropped.

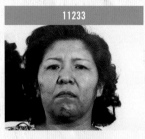

11233

WILSON, ESTELLA
Age 41, Issuing a Check Without Funds
Nez Perce County, 1963
Served 1 yr., 1 mo., 23 days

Convicted of check fraud. Wilson entered the prison with at least seven arrests for public drunkenness, disturbing the peace, and other nonviolent offenses.

3542

WILSON, WANA
Age 24, Robbery
Washington County, 1925
Served 1 yr., 7 mos., 26 days

Convicted with a male accomplice of robbing Idahoans at gunpoint. Prosecutors called her a "dope fiend" and claimed she was a well-known prostitute.

2680

WOODFINE, ANNA
Age 38, Arson
Shoshone County, 1918
Served 1 yr., 7 mos.

Convicted with her husband for setting fire to their home in Wallace. The crime, an insurance scam, spread terror throughout the fire-prone timber country.

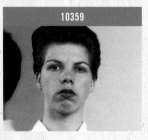

10359

WRIGHT, MYRNA LEE
Age 20, Grand Larceny
Ada County, 1959
Served 2 yrs., 9 days

Convicted for stealing cash from a neighbor's apartment. A habitual thief, Wright was said to steal "anything she could get her hands on."

5444

YATES, LUELLA
Age 42, Manslaughter, Involuntary
Jerome County, 1937
Served 1 yr., 2 mos., 13 days

Convicted of shooting a threatening neighbor in a dispute over livestock. Petitioners in Jerome County claimed that the shooting was in self-defense.

■ VIOLENT CRIME   ■ MORAL CRIME   ■ THEFT CRIME   ■ PETTY CRIME   ■ OTHER CRIME

Beyond museums and historic buildings, in storerooms controlled for climate and dust, are the tens of thousands of priceless objects and artworks that curators preserve on behalf of the state. Meaning adheres to these objects, but not everything can be preserved. To catalog, restore, and curate is to make lasting judgments about how the past connects to the present and what the future might come to think about Idaho's place in the world. Pictured: Sarah Phillips, curator, prepares an Idaho 1913 women's suffrage banner for display in the state museum.

SOURCE: ISHS

"It's a shame that many who have nothing in common must be placed together," wrote Nancy "Chris" Christopher, inmate no. 10101, reporting for The Clock in 1960. "How much better it would be if these incoming women could be screened and placed in their own category. . . . One thing is certain; if incarceration doesn't teach you a lesson, the everlasting moans of "Bum Beef," "Poor Me," and "Injustice" will." Pictured: A double-bunk Women's Ward cell.

SOURCE: ISHS

Acknowledgments

Making a book is like sailing a ship with calloused hands pulling ropes in many directions, forever readjusting the course. We thank historian Skye Cranney for the anchor of 216 original biographical essays. Beyond contributors previously listed — the editors, artists, and researchers who sailed at breakneck speed — we evened our keel with help from generous colleagues, among them Chelsee Boehm, Erin Bostwick, Angie Davis, Alisha Graefe, Danielle Grundel, Thomas Hummel, Nicole Inghilterra, Layce Johnson, Pat Truman, and Royce Williams. Thanks also to the Idaho State Historical Society, our publisher, who allowed the book to be peer reviewed so that scholars could ask hard questions, charting a course of their own.

Left: A Canadian artist reflects on a time when rebellious young women were called "incorrigible" and imprisoned for morality crimes, 2019. Chloe Cushman, *The New Yorker*

Selected Sources

The Idaho State Archives and Research Center holds the state's deepest vein of primary documentation, including transcripts, ephemera, and biographical files. Boise State University Albertsons Library archives historical photos from the *Idaho Statesman*. The University of Idaho Library also holds documentary photos and access to transcripts and papers concerning penal and criminal law. For Idaho women in the Great Depression, see the Library of Congress archive of Farm Security Administration photos; see also the library's records of the National Woman Suffrage Association and its American Women gateway to protest pamphlets and files.

Adler, Freda. *Sisters in Crime: The Rise of the New Female Criminal*. New York: McGraw-Hill, 1975.

Ancestry.com. *Historical Newspapers, Birth, Marriage, & Death Announcements, 1851-2003* (Online database). Provo, UT: Ancestry.com Operations Inc., 2006.

Ancestry.com. *Idaho, Old Penitentiary Prison Records, 1882-1961* (Online database). Lehi, UT: Ancestry.com Operations, Inc., 2017.

Ancestry.com. *U.S., Social Security Death Index, 1935-2014* (Online database). Provo, UT: Ancestry.com Operations Inc., 2014.

Beierle, Amber, Ashley Phillips, and Hanako Wakatsuki. *Images of America: Old Idaho Penitentiary*. Mt. Pleasant, SC: Arcadia Publishing, 2014.

Bordin, Ruth. *Woman and Temperance: The Quest for Power and Liberty*. Philadelphia: Temple University Press, 1981.

Butler, Anne M. *Gendered Justice in the American West: Women Prisoners in Men's Penitentiaries*. Chicago and Urbana: University of Illinois Press, 1997.

Carr, David. "Chastity and Adultery." *American Philosophical Quarterly* 23 (October 1986): 363-371.

Connelly, Mark Thomas. *The Response to Prostitution in the Progressive Era*. Chapel Hill: University of North Carolina Press, 1980.

Freedman, Estelle. *Their Sister's Keepers: Women's Prison Reform in America, 1830-1930*. Ann Arbor: University of Michigan Press, 1984.

Hayden, Erica Rhodes, and Theresa R. Jach, eds. *Incarcerated Women: A History of Struggles, Oppression, and Resistance in American Prisons*. Lanham, MD: Lexington Books, 2017.

Idaho State Board of Corrections. *The Biennial Report of the Idaho State Penitentiary*. Prepared by the Warden. Boise, ID, 1894-1968.

Idaho State Board of Corrections, Education Department. *The Clock*. Boise, ID, 1952-1968.

Idaho State Penitentiary Inmate File Collection. AR 42. Idaho State Archives, Boise, ID.

Idaho State Penitentiary Mugshot Collection. AR 42. Idaho State Archives, Boise, ID.

Idaho Statesman (Boise), 1864-1970.

Johnstone, Rachel S. *Inmates of the Idaho Penitentiary 1864-1947*. Boise: Idaho State Historical Society Press, 2009.

Kellor, Frances A. "Psychological and Environmental Study of Women Criminals I." *American Journal of Sociology* 5, no. 4 (1900): 527-543.

Lerner, Gerda. *The Creation of the Patriarchy*. New York: Oxford University Press, 1986.

Lombroso, Cesare. *The Female Offender*. New York: D. Appleton & Company, 1895.

MacGregor, Carol Lynn. *Boise, Idaho, 1882-1910: Prosperity in Isolation*. Missoula, MT: Mountain Press, 2006.

McCammon, Holly. *The U.S. Women's Jury Movement and Strategic Adaptation: A More Just Verdict*. Cambridge: Cambridge University Press, 2012.

McNeil, Joanne. "The 'White Slavery' Panic." *Reason* 39, no. 11 (April 2008): 58-61.

Meinzer, Heidi. "Idaho's Throwback to Elizabethan England: Criminalizing a Civil Proceeding." *Family Law Quarterly* 34 (Spring 2000): 165-175.

Nash, Sarah. *Women Helping Women: A Centennial History of the Boise YWCA/WCA*. Virginia Beach, VA: Donning Co. Publishers, 2011.

NewsBank (Online database). *Idaho Statesman* Current and Historical Collection. Boise Public Library, Boise, ID.

Old Penitentiary Oral History Collection, 1976-1995. Idaho State Archives, Boise, ID.

Penson-Ward, Betty. *Idaho Women in History: Big & Little Biographies and Other Gender Stories*. Boise, ID: Legendary Publishing, 1991.

Rafter, Nicole Hahn. *Partial Justice: Women in State Prisons, 1800-1935*. Boston: Northeastern University Press, 1985.

Rapaport, Elizabeth. "The Death Penalty and Gender Discrimination." *Law & Society Review* 25 (1991): 367-384.

Russell, Jo Anne. "A Necessary Evil: Prostitutes, Patriarchs & Profits in Boise City." Master's thesis, Boise State University, 1991.

Scofield, Rebecca, and Katherine G. Aiken, "Balancing Act: Idaho's Campaign for Woman Suffrage." *Western Legal History* 33 (November 2019): 33-44.

Sermon, Suzanne. "Beyond Simple Domesticity: Organizing Boise Women, 1866-1920." Master's thesis, Boise State University, 1996.

Shallat, Todd, ed. *The Other Idahoans: Forgotten Stories of the Boise Valley*. Boise: Boise State University, 2016.

Shelden, Randall G. Controlling the Criminal Classes: *A Critical Introduction to the History of Criminal Justice*. Boston: Allyn and Bacon, 2001.

Spaulding, Edith R. *An Experimental Study of Psychopathic Delinquent Women*. New York: Rand, McNally & Company, 1923.

Stacy, Susan. "Our Ward Is Rather Small." *Idaho Yesterdays* 38 (1994): 22-31.

U.S. Bureau of the Census. *Statistical Abstract of the United States: 1880, 1900, 1920, 1940, 1960*. Washington, DC: Government Printing Office.

U.S. Bureau of the Census. *Tenth–Sixteenth Census of the United States, 1880-1940*. Washington, DC: National Archives and Records Administration.

Waite, Robert G. "Necessary to Isolate the Female Prisoners: Women Convicts and the Women's Ward at the Old Idaho Penitentiary." *Idaho Yesterdays* 29 (Fall 1985): 2-12.

Western States Marriage Search Form. BYU-Idaho Special Collections and Family History. Rexburg, ID. https://abish.byui.edu/specialCollections/westernStates/search.cfm.

Wimberly, Rosemary L. "'Menaces to Society': Sex, Adultery, and Abortion Crimes of Idaho Woman Prisoners, 1900-1960." *Idaho Yesterdays* 38 (1994): 13-21.

Left: The penitentiary's wide arches inspired the brownstone architecture of Boise's Romanesque Revival. Previous: South Wing, originally housing a shoe factory; Warden's son Edward Logan Campbell under the southwest guard tower, about 1894. Following: Mother and child uprooted by dust storms in Idaho's Oneida County, 1936.

SOURCES: ISHS, Q CONCEPTS, ISHS, LIBRARY OF CONGRESS

"Why study history? The answer is because we virtually must," writes Peter Stearns, a historian of social forces that hit women harder than men. *"The past causes the present, and so the future. Only through studying history can we grasp how things change; only through history can we begin to comprehend the factors that cause change; and only through history can we understand what elements of an institution or a society persist despite change."*

Numbered: Inside Idaho's Prison for Women, 1887-1968, can be ordered via the Old Idaho Penitentiary website at history.idaho.gov. Contact the publisher for review or classroom copies at (208) 334-2844.